Shoe-Maker

Cooper

Printer

Baker

Weaver

Butcher and Cook

ROLL OF APPRENTICES
BURGH OF ABERDEEN
1622-1796

Three Parts in One Volume

1622-1699
1700-1750
1751-1796

Compiled by

Frances J. McDonnell

CLEARFIELD

Originally published
St. Andrews, Scotland
1994

Reprinted for Clearfield Company by
Genealogical Publishing Company
Baltimore, Maryland
2015

ISBN 978-0-8063-5760-7

ROLL OF APPRENTICES
BURGH OF ABERDEEN
1622-1699

INTRODUCTION

Economic and social power in medieval and early modern Scottish burghs lay in the hands of a self-perpetuating oligarchy called burgesses. The rights to operate a business and to vote were limited to these burgesses, who, in order to maintain their priviledges, operated what today would be described as a "closed shop". To become a burgess of Aberdeen, one had to be the son of an existing Aberdeen burgess, marry the daughter of a burgess, buy the right, or serve an apprenticeship under a craftsman or merchant in the burgh. For an apprentice who did not qualify on other grounds, it was of paramount importance that his apprenticeship indenture be recorded to ensure that he became entitled in due course to apply to become a burgess.

Although most Royal Burghs maintained a Register of Indentures, very vew have been transcribed and subsequently published. This booklet, laid out in alphabetical order, is based on the work of the Victorian antiquarian Alexander M Munro.

Frances J McDonnell
St Andrews
January 1994

REGISTER OF INDENTURES - BURGH OF ABERDEEN
1622 - 1699

A

Abercrombie, James   14 Feb 1684
  Son to late James Abercrombie, late Baillie of Edinburgh,
  apprenticed to Mr Mathew Mackaill, chemist surgeon, 5 years and 1
  year
Abercrombie, Robert   Apr 1637
  Son to Robert Abercrombie in Birnes, apprenticed to Paul Inglis,
  merchant, 4 years and 1 year
Adam, Andrew   29 Aug 1667
  Apprenticed to John Christie, merchant, 4 years from 16 May 1666
Adam, Gilbert   29 Aug 1655
  Third son to George Adam in Maryculter, apprenticed to George
  Adam, weave, 5 years and 1 year
Adame, George   16 Feb 1638
  Son to George Adame, in Bakwall, apprenticed to James Malice,
  weaver, 7 years and 1 year
Alexander, John   30 Jan 1649
  Apprenticed to Archibald Hog, shoemaker, 5 years and 1 year
Allardes, William   16 Sep 1653
  Son to Mr David Allardes, sometime minister of Otris in Caithness,
  apprenticed to Alexander Charles, wright, 7 years and 2 years
Anderson, Gilbert   24 Jul 1648
  Tailor, apprenticed to John Middletoun, tailor, 6 years and 1 year
Anderson, Gilbert   1 Jan 1659
  Son to John Anderson in Kinerine, apprenticed to William Shand, late
  treasurer, 4 years and 1 year
Anderson, James   5 Jul 1632
  Son to Mr Walter Anderson, minister of Kinellar, to William Forbes,
  elder, burgess of Aberdeen, for 5 years
Anderson, John   17 Dec 1639
  Son to late William Anderson sometime at the kirk of Alford,
  apprenticed to David Nicolson, weaver, 6 years and 1 year
Anderson, Thomas   12 Dec 1662
  Son to Mr William Anderson, apprenticed to Andrew Cragheid, 6
  years and 1 year, indenture 4 Apr 1661

1

Aberdeen Apprenticeships

Anderson, William   1 Dec 1647
Son to Thomas Anderson of Auchaballa, apprenticed to Mr Robert Farquhar of Mowny, late provost of Aberdeen, 5 years

Anderson, William   18 Dec 1649
Son to Thomas Anderson of Arhabala, apprenticed to Mr Robert Farquhar of Mownie, 5 years (Martinmas 1647)

Arbuckles, James   23 May 1662
Son to James Arbuckles, merchant, burgess of Edinburgh, apprenticed to John Super, merchant, 5 years from Whitsunday 1661

Archibald, David   11 Sep 1678
Son to William Archibald sometime in Gilcomstoun, apprenticed to Walter Archibald, butcher, 6 years and 1 year

Archibald, William   11 Jan 1655
Son to the late David Archibald in Clerkseatt, apprenticed to John Ord, burgess, 4 years and 1 year, from Whitsunday 1653

Atholl, James   8 Feb 1628
Son to late Thomas Atholl, burgess to Alexander Blair, tailor, 7 years and 1 year

B

Baird, Gilbert   16 May 1654
Son to Gilbert Baird in Laynyeat, apprenticed to James Dowe, tailor, 8 years and 1 year

Barclay, John   1 Jan 1659
Son of the late Mr Patrick Barclay, minister at Keig, apprenticed to John Gray, saddler, 4 years from 28 Sep 1658

Bartlet, Alexander   7 Apr 1675
Son to William Bartlet in Robslaw, apprenticed to James Bartlet, merchant, 6 years

Baverlay, George   27 Sep 1649
Son to William Baverlay in Seatoun, apprenticed to Gilbert Arthur, weaver, 4 years (Jan 1648)

Baxter, George   1 Jul 1643
Son to George Baxter, dyer in Elgin, with consent of his father, apprenticed to Alexander Robertson, merchant, 4 years from Whitsunday

Bazie, William   8 Jul 1663
Eldest lawful son to the late James Bazie in Aberdeen, apprenticed to Patrick Murray, baker, 8 years and 1 year

Aberdeen Apprenticeships

Best, Thomas   24 Sep 1632
>   Younger son to late Thomas Best, burgess of Aberdeen, to Thomas
>   Best, burgess, for 5 years and 1 year

Black, Alexander   15 May 1648
>   Apprenticed to Patrick Black, saddler, 5 years and 1 year

Black, Nathaniel   9 Feb 1649
>   Brother to William Black, saddler, burgess of Aberdeen, apprenticed
>   to the said William, 5 years and 1 year from 25 Jul 1648

Black, Patrick   23 Jun 1649
>   Son to Alexander Black at the milne of Petcaple, apprenticed to
>   James Anderson, merchant, 6 years from Whitsunday 1644

Boyne, John   2 Aug 1656
>   Brother to George Boyne, burgess of Aberdeen, apprenticed to Walter
>   Melvill, goldsmith, 7 years from 29 Nov 1655

Branes, John   1 Apr 1647
>   Son to the late William Branes, shoemaker, apprenticed to James
>   Hall, shoemaker, 7 years from 10 Aug 1644

Brodie, James   10 Jun 1689
>   Son to Mr James Brodie, brother german to the Laird of Lethnie,
>   apprenticed to Mr Mathew McKaill, chemist burgess, 5 years

Brown, Alexander   18 Jan 1631
>   Son to Alexander Brown, mariner, to Robert Ross, tailor, for 6 years
>   and 1 year

Brown, Francis   27 Jul 1653
>   Brother to John Brown, burgess, apprenticed to the said John, 4
>   years, from Whitsunday 1652

Brown, James   19 Feb 1656
>   Son to Barbara Barroick in Capriston, apprenticed to Adam Smith,
>   weaver, 5 years and 1 year from 20 Nov 1654

Brown, John   25 Nov 1630
>   Son to Mr William Brown, minister at the kirk of Invernochtie, to
>   Thomas Thomson, merchant, for 4 years

Brown, John   30 Jul 1631
>   Son to late Patrick Brown, servant to George, Lord Gordon, to Thomas
>   Gairdyn, tailor, for 5 years and 1 year

Buchan, John   3 Nov 1670
>   Son to Patrick Buchan, brother german to Gilbert Buchan in the
>   Hospital of Old Aberdeen, apprenticed to James Hill, shoemaker, 4
>   years and 1 year from 10 July 1669

Burnet, Alexander   7 Oct 1647
>   Son to James Burnet in Grange, apprenticed to Gilbert Watson,
>   merchant, 4 years and 1 year

Aberdeen Apprenticeships

Burnet, Alexander   16 Sep 1650
  Son to Thomas Burnet of Campbell, apprenticed to William Leslie, elder, 5 years for learning the merchant trade, from Whitsunday 1650

Burnet, Alexander   12 Oct 1652
  Son to Alexander Burnet of Inverrie, apprenticed to Andrew ?, Burgess, 3 years

Burnet, Andrew   5 Feb 1641
  Son to Andrew Burnet of Schedockisly, apprenticed to John Donaldson, merchant, 5 years

Burnet, George   18 Feb 1652
  Son to late Robert Burnet, burgess of Aberdeen, apprenticed to John Sangster, burgess, 3 years and 1 year

Burnet, James   5 Jul 1672
  Son to Mr William Burnet minister at Inch, apprenticed to Mr Mathew Mackale, chemist, 5 years

Burnet, Patrick   21 Dec 1654
  Son of James Burnet in Grange, apprenticed to William Shand, burgess, 4 years and 1 year from Whitsunday 1653

Burnett, Andrew   10 Jan 1672
  Son to the late Alexander Burnett in Newtoune of Premnay, apprenticed to James Byres, burgess, 5 years from Martinmas 1670

C

Cargill, James   1 Feb 1649
  Apprenticed to Patrick Blair, 4 years

Carle, William   15 Dec 1662
  Son to the late James Carle, resident in Aberdeen, apprenticed to William Cruickshank, armourer, 4 years and 1 year

Carmichaell, James   22 Aug 1648
  Apprenticed to Malcolm Wilson, hammerman, 4 years and 1 year

Carnegie, James   12 Sep 1653
  Son to William Carnegie in Pitfrass, apprenticed to Charles Dun, dyer, 7 years from 2 Jun 1650

Cassie, Richard   9 Feb 1622
  Son to late John Cassie in Hazelhead, apprenticed to John Paterson, weaver for 8 years as apprentice and 2 years for meat and fee

Cattenach, John   20 Jan 1673
  Son to the late Robert Cattenach, sometime at the milne of Ardlair, apprenticed to Alexander Cragmyll, cooper, 5 years and 1 year

Aberdeen Apprenticeships

Catto, John   13 Jul 1680
Only son to William Catto at the middle milne of Kintore,
apprenticed to Alexander Craigmyll, cooper, 6 years from March
1679

Charles, James   19 Feb 1656
Son to Alexander Charles, wright, apprenticed to Alexander Charles,
wright, 6 years and 1 year

Cheine, David   13 Jul 1680
Son to the late Mr William Cheine minister at Skene, apprenticed to
Mr Mathew McKaile, surgeon, 6 years

Cheine, James   28 Feb 1659
Son to John Cheine in Old Aberdeen, apprenticed to John Strachan,
weaver, 7 years and 1 year from 9 Jun 1654

Christie, James   9 Mar 1648
Apprenticed to George Moreson, tailor, 6 years and 1 year

Christie, John   31 Jan 1665
Son to Alexander Christie in Alford, apprenticed to Patrick Christie
elder, burgess, 7 years and 1 year from Martinmas 1664

Christie, Peter   3 Oct 1659
In Brandley, apprenticed to Peter Christie, merchant, 4 years from
Whitsunday 1658

Christie, William   2 Apr 1647
Apprenticed to Alexander Ettershank, cooper, 5 years and 1 year

Clerk, James   13 Mar 1665
Lawful son to the late Thomas Clerk in Newburgh, apprenticed to
William Cruickshank, armourer, 4 years and 1 year

Clerk, John   30 May 1653
Third son to Mr James Clerk of Tillicorthie, apprenticed to George
Moresone, tailor, 5 years and 1 year from 13 Nov 1652

Clerk, John   20 May 1657
Son to Patrick Clerk, apprenticed to Andrew Chopman, baker, 6 years
and 1 year

Cluneis, Alexander   30 May 1649
Second son to Thomas Cluneis, burgess of Cromerty, apprenticed to
Alexander Farquhar, merchant, 6 years and 1 year from May 1647

Collin, James   30 Apr 1669
Son to Alesander Collin sometime in Skillimarnoch, apprenticed to
James Barclay, merchant, 7 years - indenture dated at Edinburgh and
Aberdeen, 20 April and 4 May 1668

Collinson, James   29 Sep 1670
Son to Gilbert Collinson, burgess, apprenticed to William Thomson,
cooper, 5 years and 1 year from 9 Nay 1668

Coutts, Andrew 4 Jul 1678
Apprenticed to Alexander Annand, wright, 5 years from 15 Jan 1677

Coutts, William 17 Jan 1665
Son to John Coutts, sometime at the Milne of Lesly, apprenticed to Alexander Charles, wright, 7 years and 1 year

Craig, Thomas 22 Jun 1648
Son to David Craig in Auchinclochie, apprenticed to William Maitland, smith, 6 years and 1 year

Craig, Walter 2 Jul 1657
Son to the late David Craig sometime in Ferachfield, apprenticed to John Keany, baker, 5 years and 1 year from Whitsunday 1656

Craig, William 17 Feb 1632
Son to Andrew Craig in Lochtieside of Murthell, to William Galloway, shoemaker, for 5 years

Craighead, Alexander 24 Jul 1648
Apprenticed to Alexander Norvell, weaver, 6 years and 1 year

Craigin, Alexander 25 Sep 1649
Son to George Craigin in the Rawes of Strathbogie, apprenticed for 6 years and 1 year

Cravy, James 29 Jan 1688
Son to James Cravy in Tarves, apprenticed to Walter Crage, baker, 5 years and 1 year

Cruickshank, Alexander 17 Nov 1632
Son to William Cruickshank in Aucharine, to John Maleis, cooper, for 6 years and 1 year

Cruickshank, George 26 Oct 1631
Son to Alexander Cruickshank in Pervyneis, apprenticed to James Crukshank, armourer, for 6 years and 1 year

Cruickshank, William 27 Jun 1644
In Cauldwalls, son to George Cruickshank yr, apprenticed to George Cruikshank armourer, 6 years and 1 year

Cruikshank, James 12 Mar 1647
Apprenticed to Alexander Cruikshank, cooper, 5 years and 1 year

Cruikshank, Patrick 2 Mar 1657
Son to William Cruikshank elder in Middletoun of Slains, apprenticed to Alexander Cruikshank, 5 years and 1 year from 27 May 1656

D

Dalgardno, Andrew 9 Mar 1648
Apprenticed to William Dalgardno, cooper, 4 years and 1 year

Davidson, Alexander   10 Apr 1654
> Son to Hendry Davidson in Knockinblewes, apprenticed to William
> Anderson, cooper, 6 years from Whitsunday 1652

Davidson, George   12 Sep 1653
> Son to John Davidson, tailor, apprenticed to William Smolt, weaver,
> 5 years and 1 year

Davidson, John   10 Apr 1654
> Eldest son to John Davidson, tailor, apprenticed to William Downy,
> tailor, 6 years and 1 year

Davidson, William   11 Mar 1659
> Son to the late William Davidson, weaver, apprenticed to John
> Hendry, shoemaker, 5 years and 1 year from 2 Sep 1657

Davie, John   28 May 1660
> Son in law to William Clark in Chapeltoun of Esslemont,
> apprenticed to Alexander Eterschank, cooper, 5 years and 1 year

Davy, James   31 Jul 1667
> Son to Alexander Davy, dyer, apprenticed to Alexander Ettershank,
> cooper, 6 years and 1 year

Deavie, Alexander   25 May 1632
> Son to Nicoll Deavie in Courthillocks, apprenticed to Walter
> Anderson, dyer, 4 years and 1 year

Deawine, William   24 May 1635
> Eldest son to James Deawine, workman in Aberdeen, apprenticed to
> William Sangster, weaver, 6 years and 1 year

Denoon, David   30 Sep 1693
> Son to David Denoon in Lonie in Moray, apprenticed to Mr Mathew
> Mckaile, chemist burgess, 3 years

Donald, Patrick   27 Apr 1649
> Son to late James Donald, sometime in Clayford, apprenticed to
> Alexander Liddingem, weaver, 8 years and 1 year

Douglas, Walter   25 Jun 1635
> Son to Hector Douglas in Muldarg, to Mr Robert Farquhar, baillie of
> Aberdeen, for 5 years

Downie, Alexander   11 Sep 1641
> Son to Andrew Downie in Hill of Kear, apprenticed to John Blinshell,
> weaver, 4 years and 1 year

Dun, Charles   17 Aug 1653
> Son to Charles Dun, dyer, apprenticed to Robert Ker, burgess, 5 years
> from Whitsunday, 1652

Dun, Hugh   17 Jan 1665
> Lawful son to Charles Dun, dyer, apprenticed to John Ross, 7 years

Dun, Thomas   22 Mar 1640
    Son to Richard Dun, farmer in Aberdeen, to Alexander Sangster,
    weaver, for 5 years and 1 year
Duncan, Alexander   28 Nov 1629
    To John Forbes, weaver, 5 years and 1 year
Duncan, Alexander   30 May 1653
    Son to Thomas Duncan in Kincardine o' Neill, apprenticed to John
    Edward, weaver, 5 years and 1 year from Whitsunday 1650
Duncan, George   25 Mar 1664
    In Petscow, apprenticed to John Duncan, late baillie, 5 years
Duncan, John   10 Aug 1625
    Son to Patrick Duncan in Scotstoun to William Duncan, burgess, 7
    years

                                E

Elmslie, John   9 Oct 1648
    Apprenticed to Alexander Cruikshank, cooper, 7 years and 1 year
Elphinstone, William   15 Sep 1668
    Lawful son to Robert Elphinstone in Govell, apprenticed to William
    Scott, goldsmith, 5 years and 1 year
Ettershank, John   1 Nov 1645
    Apprentice to Alexander Ettershank, 5 years and 2 years, from 17
    April 1643

                                F

Fairindaill, Robert   20 Jan 1655
    Son to Ochtrean Fairindaill, glover, apprenticed to Hugh Maghie,
    chemist, 8 years from 11 Nov 1652
Fairlie, John   11 Mar 1657
    Son to Norman Fairlie at the Kirk of Inch, apprenticed to John Gray,
    saddler, 4 years and 1 year from 24 Sep 1656
Fans, John   13 May 1674
    Son to late Alexander Fans in Belskewie, apprenticed to John
    Archbald, merchant, 5 years and 1 year
Farquhar, Alexander   26 Apr 1641
    Son to Gilbert Farquhar in Whytwell, apprenticed to James Anderson,
    merchant, 3 years after Whitsunday, 1640

Farquhar, George   8 Jun 1630
> Son to late Findlay Farquhar in Cors to Mr Robert Farquhar, burgess,
> for 3 years

Farquhar, George   23 Feb 1656
> Son to the late James Farquhar in Banchory, apprenticed to Patrick
> Murray, shoemaker, 5 years and 1 year from Lammas 1654

Farquhar, John   22 Oct 1638
> Son to Gilbert Farquhar in Whytwell of Brecko, apprenticed to
> William Ronaldson, merchant, 3 years after Whitsunday, 1639

Farquhar, Robert   24 Apr 1656
> Son to Alexander Farquhar of Banchory, apprenticed to Alexander
> Jaffray of Kingswells, 5 years from Martinmas last

Fergusson, Alexander   4 Jul 1678
> Son to Mr John Fergusson minister at Glenmuick, apprenticed to
> Patrick Chrystie, elder, merchant, 5 years and 1 year

Fettes, William   9 Jun 1632
> Son to David Fettes in Auchmull, to James Nicoll, shoemaker, for 4
> years and 1 year

Fiddes, John   14 May 1652
> Son to late Thomas Fiddes, resident in Aberdeen, apprenticed to
> George Moresoune, tailor, 7 years and 1 year from Lammas 1649

Findlay, George   24 Jul 1652
> Patrick Findlay produced indenture wherein his son George was
> apprenticed to Alexander Mill, shoemaker, for 5 years and 1 year

Forbes, Alexander   15 Sep 1668
> Son to Alexander Forbes sometime in Lesly, apprenticed to William
> Scott, goldsmith, 6 years and 1 year

Forbes, Alexander   31 Oct 1673
> Son to William Forbes of Tombege, apprenticed to Adam Smith,
> merchant, 3 years

Forbes, Alexander   31 Oct 1673
> Second son to Alexander Forbes of Auchorthies, apprenticed to John
> Skeen, merchant, 6 years

Forbes, James   10 Jan 1672
> Son to William Forbes in Watson, apprenticed to Andrew Chopman,
> baker, 5 years and 1 year from Feb 1670

Forbes, James   11 Sep 1678
> Youngest son to John Forbes of Leslie, apprenticed to Robert
> Cruikshank yr, merchant, 5 years

Forbes, John   24 Aug 1652
> Son to Arthur Forbes in Kinknok, apprenticed to John Frobes, younger,
> merchant, 5 years from Martinmas 1649

Aberdeen Apprenticeships

Forbes, John   24 Jan 1658
> Son to John Forbes, stationer, apprenticed to James Browne, printer, 2 years from 23 Nov 1657

Forbes, John   1 Dec 1671
> Son to John Forbes in Elrick, apprenticed to John Souper, merchant, 5 years from 23 Nov 1670

Forbes, Patrick   7 May 1679
> Son to William Forbes of New, apprenticed to John Archibald, merchant, 5 years from Jun 1678

Forbes, Walter   16 Jun 1648
> Son to Mr William Forbes of Tilliegrig, apprenticed to John Donaldson younger, 4 years and 1 year

Forbes, William   25 Mar 1664
> Son to Arthur Forbes in Ogie, apprenticed to Alexander Cruickshank, cooper, 6 years and 1 year from Whitsunday 1663

Forsyth, Alexander   27 May 1643
> Apprenticed to James Strachan, cooper, 5 years and 1 year

Forsyth, John   1 Dec 1655
> Son to John Forsyth in Aberdeen, apprenticed to Alexander Telly, shoemaker, 5 years and 1 year

Fraser, Hugh   26 Jun 1689
> Second son to David Fraser of Moune, apprenticed to Mr Mathew McKaill, chemist in Aberdeen, 5 years

Fyff, George   4 Aug 1663
> Son to George Fyff, merchant in Aberdeen, apprenticed to Patrick Murray, baker, 5 years and 1 year from 18 May 1661

G

Garioch, Alexander   10 May 1655
> Son to Mr Alexander Garioch, minister at Peterculter, apprenticed to Andrew Watson, merchant, 5 years from 1 Dec 1654

Garioch, John   14 Feb 1648
> Son to late Alexander Garioch, butcher, apprenticed to George Adam, weaver, 5 years and 1 year

Garro, Robert   4 Mar 1641
> Son to Alexander Garro in Ordbodie, apprenticed to David Nicolson, weaver, 4 years and 1 year

Geddes, David   14 Dec 1635
> Son to John Geddes in the Mont, to James Geddes, tailor, for 5 years and 1 year

Geddes, Gilbert   12 Mar 1655
Son to George Geddes, mariner, apprenticed to Peter Shirres, shoemaker, 6 years and 1 year from Whitsunday 1653

Gellan, John   12 Jun 1658
Son to Robert Gellan, butcher, apprenticed to Alexander Branes, butcher, 5 years and 1 year from 26 Jan 1658

Gellie, Patrick   7 May 1679
Son to Mr John Gellie minister at Kinkell, apprenticed to James Bartlet, merchant, 4 years

Gerard, Robert   7 Apr 1662
Son to James Gerard in Rochmackinthie, apprenticed to Alexander Jaffray of Kingswalls 4 years

Gerrard, William   17 Feb 1670
Brother german to Robert Gerrard burgess, apprenticed to the said Robert, 4 years from 10 August 1668

Gib, William   1 Mar 1648
Son to William Gib in Tillifour, apprenticed to Thomas Davidson, tailor, 5 years and 1 year

Gibboun, John   3 Apr/9 Jun 1637
Son to John Gibboun in Lumphanan, to John Duncan, elder, burgess of Aberdeen, for 5 years and 1 year

Gilruiff, James   28 Jul 1663
Son to Alexander Gilruiff in Gilcomstoun, apprenticed to John Archbald, burgess, 4 years

Glenny, James   2 Mar 1657
Son to the late John Glenny at the Barkmill, apprenticed to Thomas Davidson, tailor, 5 years and 1 year

Glenny, Robert   23 Nov 1642
Apprenticed to Magnus Robertson, 8 years and 2 years

Gleny, William   1 Apr 1647
Son to John Gleny in Balllquhyne, apprenticed to John Ritchie, cooper, 5 years and 1 year from 1 Jan 1646

Gordon, George   28 Sep 1659
Son to Alexander Gordon, late ballie in Aberdeen, apprenticed to Robert Leslie, merchant, 5 years and 1 year

Gordon, James   22 Dec 1654
Son to John Gordon in Kellie, apprenticed to George Pyper, merchant, 7 years

Gordon, John   13 Apr 1647
Son to James Gordon, apprenticed to late James Rany, shoemaker, 6 years and 1 year from 2 Dec 1640

Gordon, Patrick   16 Jul 1653
> Son to the late Robert Gordon, tailor, apprenticed to Willian Gordon, tailor, 5 years and 1 year

Gordon, William   27 Jul 1653
> Son to the late James Gordon, mason, apprenticed to William Gray, weaver, 5 years and 2 years

Gray, Alexander   5 May 1639
> Son to Archibald Gray in Portlethen, to George Jollie, weaver, for 5 years and 1 year

Gray, Alexander   25 Aug 1648
> Apprenticed to William Gray, weaver, 5 years and 1 year

Gray, Andrew   1 Apr 1647
> Son to Andrew Gray in Mondurno, apprenticed to Alexander Gray, cooper, 5 years and 1 year from 2 Jun 1642

Gray, Andrew   1 Sep 1654
> Second son to Andrew Gray at the Mill of Mondurno, apprenticed to Alexander Ettershank, cooper, 5 years and 1 year

Gray, Patrick   17 Nov 1652
> Son to Andrew Gray at the milne of Mondurno, apprenticed to John Malice, cooper, 5 years and 1 year, from Candlemas 1653

Gregory, David   29 Apr 1643
> Son to Mr John Gregorie, minister at Drumoak with consent of his father, apprenticed to John Donaldson elder, burgess, 5 years

Grige, Thomas   27 May 1657
> Lawful son to David Grige in Auchlunes, apprenticed to Thomas Ritchie, weaver, 5 years and 1 year, from 19 Nov 1656

Guidaill, John   3 Jan 1644
> Son to John Guidaill, apprenticed to Peter Shirres, shoemaker, 6 years from Whitsunday, 1641

H

Hall, Alexander   11 Dec 1663
> Son to James Hall, apprenticed to James Robertson yr, 5 years

Hardie, Robert   24 Jul 1652
> Son to Alexander Hardie, Meikle Tibbertie, apprenticed to Alexander Robertson, merchant, 6 years from Whitsunday 1649

Harvie, Alexander   1 Aug 1663
> Son to Thomas Harvie in Tillielt, apprenticed to Alexander Charles, wright, 4 years

Aberdeen Apprenticeships

Hay, Andrew   11 Feb 1670
> Son to James Hay, resident in Aberdeen, apprenticed to George Fyfe, baker, 5 years and 1 year from 22 Feb 1669

Hay, Andrew   11 Feb 1670
> Brother to William Hay, merchant burgess, apprenticed to the said William, 3 years

Hay, Robert   29 Aug 1667
> Lawful son to William Hay in Stonefield, apprenticed to John Duncan, baillie of Aberdeen, 6 years from Whitsunday 1666

Hedderwick, John   1 Sep 1668
> Son to Andrew Hedderwick, resident in Aberdeen, apprenticed to Andrew Cragheid, butcher, 6 years and 1 year

Hog, Archibald   29 Oct 1636
> Son to William Hog in Knappath, to James Hill, shoemaker, for 5 years and 1 year

Hog, James   2 Oct 1646
> Son to the late William Hog in Knapach, apprenticed to Archibald Hog, shoemaker, 5 years and 1 year from 21 Jun 1646

Howeson, William   1 May 1655
> Son to the late Marin Howeson in Aberdeen, apprenticed to William Gordon, tailor, 6 years and 1 year

Hunter, Samuel   8 Sep 1649
> Son to James Hunter, sometime in Oykhorn, apprenticed to late William Anderson, cooper, 5 years (Whitsunday, 1641)

Hutcheon, William   7 Jul 1648
> Apprenticed to John Leslie, weaver, 6 years and 1 year

I

Idle, Alexander   16 Apr 1661
> Son to Alexander Idle in Culter Cullen, apprenticed to Thomas Yull, shoemaker, 3 years from 9 Aug 1660

Innes, Alexander   10 Jan 1648
> Son to late George Innes, apprenticed to Patrick Murray, baker, 5 years and 1 year

Innes, Alexander   18 Dec 1649
> Son to George Innes in Carterfauldie, apprenticed to Patrick Murray, baker, 5 years and 1 year (10 Jan 1648)

J

Jack, James   31 Mar 1647
>Apprenticed to William Davidson, weaver, 6 years and 1 year

Jamieson, John   1 Jan 1646
>Son to Gilbert Jamieson in Old Meldrum, apprenticed to John Donaldson yr, burgess, 5 years from 26 Dec 1645

Jamieson, William   4 Nov 1648
>Apprenticed to George Farquhar, merchant, 6 years and 1 year

Johne, Hendrie   11 Jan 1655
>Son in Law to Alexander Alexander in Brae of Pitfoddell, apprenticed to Robert Sangster, weaver, 5 years and 1 year from Whitsunday 1655

Johnstone, Alexander   21 Dec 1654
>Son to George Johnstone, merchant in Old Deer, apprenticed to James Ewan, burgess, 7 years

Johnstone, Alexander   2 Oct 1655
>Son in law to William Taylor, resident, apprenticed to Samuel Hunter, cooper, 7 years and 1 year

Johnstone, John   29 Jan 1688
>Eldest lawful son to John Johnstone of Newplace, apprenticed to Thomas Mitchell, late baillie, 5 years

Jois, James   2 Aug 1653
>Apprenticed to Alexander George younger, smith, 4 years and 1 year

K

Kay, George   23 Jul 1656
>Son of the late Thomas Kay, farmer in Aberdeen, apprenticed to Patrick Murray, baker, 5 years and 1 year from 22 Jan 1656

Keith, Gilbert   1 Aug 1657
>Son to the late John Keith sometime kirk officer at Skene, apprenticed to William Davidson, weaver, 5 years and 1 year from 2 Dec 1652

Keith, John   3 Aug 1653
>Son to Alexander Keith, farmer, apprenticed to Patrick Murray, shoemaker, ? years and 1 year from 18 May 1652

Kemptie, William   3 Feb 1644
>Son to the late George Kemptie at the Milne of Gourdes, apprenticed to William Scott in Fyvie, merchant burgess of Aberdeen, 5 years from Martinmas 1643

Aberdeen Apprenticeships

Kenny, John   14 May 1634
> Son to late John Kenny, sometime baker burgess of Arbroath, to
> John Middletoun, baker, for 5 years

King, Robert   22 Jan 1658
> Lawful son to John King, burgess of Aberdeen, apprenticed to
> Alexander Charles, carpenter, 5 years and 2 years

Kinneir, Andrew   28 Jul 1663
> Son to James Kinneir in Bogjargin, apprenticed to John Archbald,
> merchant, 5 years and 1 year

L

Lamb, George   26 Feb 1656
> Son to the late William Lamb, baker in Aberdeen, apprenticed to
> Alexander Innes, baker, 6 years and 1 year

Law, Duncan   28 Aug 1654
> Lawful brother to Robert Law, merchant in Old Aberdeen, apprenticed
> to Alexander Black, saddler, 6 years and 1 year

Law, Robert   12 Apr 1653
> Brother german to John Law, wright, burgess, apprenticed to the said
> John Law, 6 years from Martinmas 1644

Leask, Gilbert   24 Mar 1664
> Son to Mr Alexander Leask, minister at Maryculter, apprenticed to
> Walter Melvill, goldsmith, 7 years

Leddikin, Alexander   26 May 1636
> Son to John Leddikin, apprenticed to Alexander Robertson, weaver, 8
> years and 1 year

Leith, John   7 Apr 1647
> Son to David Leith in Carnetoish, apprenticed to Patrick Leith, tailor,
> 6 years and 1 year from 2 Feb 1647

Leonard, Alexander   13 Jul 1680
> Son to Walter Leonard at the Bridge of Dee, apprenticed to Alexander
> Gellan, butcher, 7 years and 1 year from Nov 1673

Leslie, Alexander   22 Feb 1670
> Son to the late Robert Leslie of Edintor, apprenticed to John
> Chrystie, merchant, 5 years from 11 March 1669

Leslie, George   25 Jan 1647
> Eldest son to James Leslie in Tilbouries, apprenticed to Patrick
> Leslie, late baillie, 5 years from 1 Feb 1647

Leslie, George   29 Nov 1649
> Son to John Leslie in Auchleawin, apprenticed to James Leslie,
> tailor, 6 years and 1 year

Leslie, James   14 Jul 1641
    Apprenticed to Magnus Robertson, 7 years and 1 year
Leslie, James   30 Mar 1684
    Son to late William Leslie of Warthill, apprenticed to James Byres,
    merchant, 5 years from 1 Jan 1680
Leslie, Lancelot   1 Jul 1643
    Son to William Leslie in Bervie with consent of his father,
    apprenticed to George Davidson, elder, burgess, 6 years from 8 Dec
    1642
Levingstoun, William   24 Dec 1669
    Son to David Levingstoun in Dunlope, apprenticed to Robert
    Cruikshank yr, merchant, 5 years
Leynord, Gilbert   1 May 1656
    Son to David Leynord in Fidie of Ord, apprenticed to Alexander
    Gordon, weaver, 6 years and 1 year from 30 Jun 1649
Leyth, George   16 May 1630
    Son to late Thomas Leyth, resident in Aberdeen, to William Forbes,
    weaver, for 7 years
Lightoun, William   12 Mar 1655
    Son to late William Lightoun in Cragwall Pittodrie, apprenticed to
    William Thomson, cooper, 6 years and 1 year from 18 Jun 1651
Lindsay, George   29 Sep 1670
    Lawful son to the late William Lindsay, sometime at the Kirk of
    Keig, apprenticed to George Lindsay, merchant, 4 years and 1 year
Lithcow, Thomas   30 Nov 1631
    Son to late John Lithcow, mason, to Thomas Gardyn, tailor, for 5
    years and 1 year
Logan, William   28 Feb 1663
    Son to Allester Logan, apprenticed to Thomas Gray, wright, 5 years
    and 1 year
Low, John   12 Mar 1659
    Son to the late James Low in Old Aberdeen, apprenticed to Andrew
    Watson, butcher, 7 years from Whitsunday 1655
Lucas, John   26 Dec 1630
    Son to late James Lucas in Hazelhead to William Smith, tailor, for 7
    years and 1 year
Lumsden, John   10 Jul 1652
    Lawful son to late Hendry Lumsden at the Bridge of Don, apprenticed
    to Alexander Harthill, merchant, 4 years and 1 year from 20 Feb
    1647
Lyall, Patrick   2 Jul 1655
    Son to John Lyall in Ferrinhill, apprenticed to Patrick Watson, dyer,
    4 years and 1 year from Martinmas 1654

M

Machray, Alexander   5 Feb 1650
>   Apprenticed to Alexander Ettershank, 10 years from Whitsunday
>   1649

Mackenzie, Alexander   12 Aug 1655
>   Son to Mr Murdo Mackenzie, minister at Elgin, apprenticed to Sir
>   Robert Farquhar of Mouny, Knight, 5 years from Martinmas 1654

Mackie, Robert   21 Jan 1632
>   Son to John Mackie in Aberdeen, to Robert Milne, shoemaker, for 5
>   years and 1 year

Mackie, William   16 Aug 1654
>   Son to the late John Mackie in Auchorsk, apprenticed to Alexander
>   Mackie, shoemaker, 5 years and 1 year

Malcolm, James   31 Jan 1665
>   Son to the late James Malcolm in Boghead, apprenticed to Patrick
>   Leith, tailor, 8 years

Manson, Alexander   21 Sep 1658
>   Eldest lawful son to Alexander Manson, resident in Aberdeen,
>   apprenticed to Dr James Lesly, doctor of medicine, 9 years from 4
>   Sept

Mark, Adam   2 Jul 1675
>   Apprenticed to Alexander Charles, wright, 4 years and 1 year from
>   Jun 1674

Marr, Hendry   May 1668
>   Son to William Marr in Peterhead, apprenticed to Alexander Charles,
>   wright, 4 years

Marr, John   29 Aug 1667
>   Son to John Marr, apprenticed to William Smoult, weaver, 6 years
>   from Whitsunday 1666

Marr, Richard   11 Jun 1649
>   Son to James Marr, burgess of Aberdeen, apprentice to Charles
>   Robertson, merchant, 5 years from Whitsunday 1648

Mathewson, Andrew   1 Aug 1656
>   Son to George Mathewson in Aberdeen, apprenticed to John Lamb,
>   weaver, 8 years and 1 year from 3 Jul 1654

Mathewson, Thomas   30 Apr 1669
>   Son to George Mathewson, farmer in Aberdeen, apprenticed to George
>   Adam, weaver, 5 years and 1 year - indenture 27 Feb 1665

Mathewson, William   20 Jan 1673
>   Son to George Mathewson in Aberdeen, apprenticed to Andrew
>   Matthewson, weaver, 8 years and 1 year from 1 Jan 1669

Aberdeen Apprenticeships

Mearns, David   12 Feb 1656
    Son to David Mearns in Inverbervie, apprenticed to Alexander
    Hutcheon, weaver, 4 years
Measson, Alexander   28 Jul 1648
    Apprenticed to Thomas Walker, shoemaker, 5 years and 1 year
Meassone, Alexander   7 May 1679
    Son to Gilbert Meassone, horse hirer, apprenticed to John Clerk,
    baker, 5 years and 1 year
Melvill, Abraham   10 Apr 1635
    Son to late John Melvill, farmer in Aberdene, apprenticed to William
    Nicolson, weaver, 5 years and 1 year
Melvill, David   23 May 1662
    Son to the late David, resident in Aberdeen, apprenticed to William
    Downy, tailor, 6 years and 1 year
Menzies, Alexander   15 Dec 1645
    Servant to George Gawin, Writer in Edinburgh, apprenticed to
    William Duffus, wright, 6 years and 1 year, from Martinmas 1645
Mercer, James   6 Oct 1655
    Son to Thomas Mercer in Ythie, apprenticed to Alexander Moir, baker,
    7 years and 1 year
Merser, Alexander   21 Sep 1648
    Apprenticed to George Moresone, tailor, 5 years
Merser, John   17 Mar 1653
    Son to John Merser in Findyeauch, apprenticed to John Middleton,
    tailor, 6 years and 1 year from 1 Aug 1651
Mershall, Alexander   11 Feb 1670
    Son to late Alexander Mershell at Barkmill, apprenticed to Walter
    Archibald, butcher, 5 years from 6 June 1668
Middleton, Andrew   19 Feb 1656
    Son to Samuel Middleton of Berriehillock, apprenticed to William
    Gray, saddler, 4 years and 1 year from Martinmas 1653
Middleton, John   1 Sep 1652
    Son of Samuel Middleton of Berriehillock, apprenticed to John
    Ritchie, cooper, 6 years and 1 year
Middleton, Samuel   15 Sep 1653
    Son to Samuel Middleton of Berriehillock, apprenticed to John
    Middleton, tailor, 6 years and 1 year
Midltoune, Alexander   13 Mar 1665
    Son to Robert Midltoune of Bordland, apprenticed to George Ross,
    pewterer, 6 years
Mill, George   11 Dec 1646
    Son to John Milne, apprenticed to Archibald Baxter, 4 years and 1
    year

18

Milne, Alexander   6 Jun 1631
    To John Blindshell, weaver for 6 years and 1 year
Milne, Alexander   5 Feb 1650
    Apprenticed to Andrew Young, 5 years and 1 year from Martinmas,
    1649
Milne, John   24 Jul 1646
    Son to Thomas Milne, apprenticed to Gilbert Malcolm, weaver, 5
    years from 7 Jun 1644
Milne, John   19 Feb 1659
    Son to William Milne at the Bridge of Dee, apprenticed to Alexander
    Milne, cooper, 6 years and 1 year
Moir, Alexander   1 Sep 1668
    Son to William Moir at Bairty, apprenticed to Robert Moir, dyer, 7
    years and 1 year - indenture 23 May 1662
Moir, Robert   6 Apr 1640
    In Aberdeen apprenticed to Andrew Meldrum, dyer, 6 years and 1 year
Moir, Thomas   15 Jan 1641
    Son to late Andrew Moir in Kintore, apprenticed to John Malice,
    cooper, 8 years and 1 year (indenture dated 28 June 1633)
Morreson, William   18 Jun 1661
    Brother to Gilbert Moreson of Bogny, apprenticed to Andrew Gudaill,
    5 years
Moutray, John (yr)   1 Aug 1663
    Apprenticed to Walter Menzies, glover, 6 years - indenture 29 Jun
    1661
Muireson, William   11 Nov 1631
    Son to Andrew Muireson in Easter Tilboureis, to John Malice, weaver,
    for 5 years and 1 year
Murdo, Alexander   2 May 1636
    Son to George Murdo in Daviot, to Magnus Robertson, wright, for 6
    years and 1 year
Murray, Francis   16 Jul 1655
    Son to Gilbert Murray, shoemaker, apprenticed to William Gray,
    weaver, 6 years and 1 year
Murray, James   23 Jun 1649
    Son to John Murray, elder, in Turriff, apprenticed to James Anderson,
    merchant, 5 years
Murray, James   27 Dec 1651
    Son to the late James Murray in Shethtie of Strachan, apprenticed to
    John Ross, merchant, 4 years and 1 year from 1 Mar 1648

Murray, Patrick   18 Mar 1640
    Son to John Murray, shoemaker in Futtie, apprenticed to Andrew
    Kellie younger, baker, 5 years and 1 year.   Ordained by the
    Magistrates to be booked "notwithstanding that the same was not
    produced within the time prescribed by the acts set down for
    booking of apprentices because the said Patrick was at that time in
    the country's service in England in the company sent out by the town
    under the Earl Marshall's regiment."
Murray, Robert   15 Oct 1646
    Son to John Murray in Loirstoun, apprenticed to John Gray, weaver, 4
    years and 1 year
Mylne, John   23 Apr 1629
    Son to John Mylne, vicar of Maryculter, to Patrick Black, saddler,
    for 6 years and 1 year
Mylne, William   10 Feb 1642
    Son to late John Mylne sometime at the Mylnes of Drum, apprenticed
    to Andrew Smith and John Smith his son, blacksmith and the longest
    lived of each, 5 years and 1 year from Candlemas, 1642

N

Nairn, James   8 Nov 1652
    Natural son to John Nairn in Ragley, apprenticed to William Sangster,
    weaver, 6 years and 2 years
Naughtie, James   27 Dec 1651
    Eldest lawful son to George Naughtie, salmon fisher, resident in
    Aberdeen, apprenticed to Andrew Young, cooper, 7 years and 1 year
    from Whitsunday 1650
Neilson, William   10 Jun 1652
    Brother german to Thomas Neilson, merchant burgess of Dornachie,
    apprenticed to George Moresoun, tailor, 5 years and 1 year
Nicoll, William   20 Jul 1641
    Son to John Nicoll in Persie, apprenticed to Robert Nicoll, merchant,
    5 years after Whitsunday, 1641
Norrie, John   31 Aug 1636
    Brother to James Norie, tailor, to Patrick Norie, tailor, for 6 years
    and 1 year

Aberdeen Apprenticeships

O

Ochterlony, David   27 Mar 1678
    Son to Mr David Ochterlony minister at Fordoun, apprenticed to
    Charles Dune, late Deane of Guild, 5 years
Ogilvie, James   31 May 1659
    Son to James Ogilvy of Westhall, apprenticed to Alexander Harthill,
    merchant, 6 years and 1 year from 17 Sep 1653
Ord, John   3 Aug 1638
    Son to late Walter Ord, sometyme in Shellertown of Ord, apprenticed
    to William Ord, wright, for 7 years and 1 year
Orem, Alexander   17 Feb 1674
    Son to William Orem in Blairdaffe, apprenticed to Patrick Chrystie
    yr, merchant, 5 years
Orum, Alexander   29 Jan 1674
    Son to the late John Orum in Dulaye, apprenticed to Robert Gerard,
    merchant, 5 years

P

Peddie, John   14 Nov 1650
    Son to late Robert Peddie sometime in Fetterkerie, apprenticed to
    Thomas Garden, tailor, 5 years and 1 year from Whitsunday 1649
Peirie, John   11 Sep 1641
    Apprenticed to John Maleis, cooper, 5 years
Peirie, William   22 Nov 1649
    Son to Thomas Peirie in Smiddietoun of Braknay, apprenticed to
    James Ronald, merchant, 4 years
Peirie, William   1 Aug 1663
    Son to William Peirie in Grange in the shire of Banff, apprenticed to
    James Byres, merchant, 4 years from 1 Apr 1661
Petrie, James   10 Mar 1669
    Son to James Petrie in Milne of Drumwhindle, apprenticed to Patrick
    Gray, cooper, 5 years and 1 year
Philp, George   13 Jul 1680
    Son to George Philp in Brae of Pitfoddels, apprenticed to James
    Shand, cooper, 6 years from May 1679
Proctor, Robert   20 Jan 1642
    Son to Robert Proctor at the Bridge of Don, apprenticed to James
    Hall, shoemaker, 6 years and 1 year

Pyper, Alexander   12 Feb 1672
    Son to late Andrew Pyper in Fordyce, apprenticed to Alexander
    Pyper, merchant, 4 years and 1 year
Pyper, Michael   14 Feb 1648
    Apprenticed to George Pyper his brother, 4 years, in terms of
    indenture dated May 1647

R

Rait, James   13 Aug 1655
    Son to George Rait in Meikle Folla, apprenticed to Andrew Rait, 3
    years from Whitsunday 1654
Ramsay, Alexander   15 Mar 1655
    Lawful son to the late James Ramsay in Craige, apprenticed to
    Robert Still, weaver, 4 years and 1 year from Martinmas 1654
Ray, George   Mar 1631
    Son to late Alexander Ray, farmer in Aberdeen, to Robert Irving,
    cooper for 6 years and 1 year
Ray, James   21 Jun 1630
    To Edward Walker, baker, for 5 years and 1 year
Reid, Alexander   29 Dec 1641
    Third son to Patrick Reid of Endurno apprenticed to Alexander
    Farquhar, merchant, 7 years from Whitsunday, 1642
Reid, William   31 Jul 1641
    Son to Patrick Reid, Collielaw, apprenticed to James Davidson,
    weaver, 5 years and 1 year
Riauch, Alexander   26 Apr 1656
    Son to Duncan Riauch in Tullioch, apprenticed to John Hendry elder,
    shoemaker, 4 years and 1 year
Riauch, James   14 Oct 1646
    Son to Duncan Riauch in Tillioch, apprenticed to Robert Leslie,
    weaver, 6 years and 1 year from 13 Jul 1644
Ritchie, Andrew   12 Jan 1648
    Son to Patrick Ritchie in Peterhead, apprenticed to Walter Cochran,
    baillie, 6 years
Ritchie, David   6 May 1643
    Apprenticed to John Ritchie, cooper, 5 years and 1 year
Robertson, Alexander   7 Jul 1665
    Son to David Robertson in Legart, apprenticed to George Robertson in
    Spittell, burgess of Aberdeen, 5 years and 1 year

Robertson, James   14 Feb 1634
    Son to late Johne Robertson sometime in Findon, apprenticed to
    George Jollie, weaver, 6 years and 1 year
Robertson, William   4 May 1652
    Eldest lawful son to James Robertson in Powcreik, apprenticed to
    John Hendrie, elder and younger, shoemakers, 4 years and 1 year.
    Indenture produced by John Robertson, notary public
Robertson, William   27 May 1659
    Son to Alexander Robertson at New Deer, apprenticed to Andrew
    Watson, butcher, 4 years from 15 Jan 1659
Rodgie, John   24 Aug 1636
    Son to late James Rodgie in Pitmurkie, to Andrew Burnett elder,
    merchant, for 5 years
Rose, David   10 Mar 1669
    Third lawful son to Hugh Rose of Clava, apprenticed to John Rose,
    merchant burgess, 5 years
Ross, Alexander   3 Apr 1666
    Lawful son to the late Alexander Ross, sometime at the mill of
    Coull, apprenticed to George Ross, pewterer, 6 years from Martinmas
    1665
Ross, Charles   10 May 1682
    Second son to Francis Ross elder of Auchlossen, apprenticed to Adam
    Smith, merchant, 4 years
Ross, John   8 May 1656
    Lawful son to the late Walter Ross, sometime in Lochtoun,
    apprenticed to John Smith, merchant burgess, 7 years and 1 year
    from Martinmas 1655
Ross, Robert   26 Apr 1648
    Apprenticed to William Duffus, wright, 8 years and 1 year
Ross, William   14 May 1652
    Brother to John Ross, burgess, apprenticed to the said John, 4 years
    and 1 year

S

Sangster, John   4 Sep 1643
    Eldest son to William Sangster, burgess, apprenticed to Mr Alexander
    Jaffray of Kingswells, 4 years
Sangster, John   29 Sep 1670
    Son to William Sangster, mason, apprenticed to Alexander Charles,
    wright, 6 years and 1 year from 17 March 1669

Scott, James   17 Feb 1674
> Son to Alexander Scott, barber, apprenticed to John Scott, carpenter, 6 years and 1 year

Scrimgeor, William   15 May 1666
> Lawful son to William Scrimgeor, cooper, apprenticed to his said father, 5 years and 1 year

Scrogie, John   5 May 1655
> Son to James Scrogie in Picktillam, apprenticed to James Wentoun, weaver, 7 years from Whitsunday 1653

Scrogie, Robert   25 Sep 1651
> Son to John Scrogie in Tilligarmouth, apprenticed to John Smith, 7 years and 1 year from Whitsunday 1648

Seaton, John   22 Sep 1646
> Son to John Seaton, apprenticed to John Midletoun, tailor, 10 years and 1 year from 9 Jul 1645

Seaton, John   28 Sep 1655
> Son to the late Robert Seaton in Spoutshouse of ?, apprenticed to George Cruickshank, burgess, 5 years

Selbie, Alexander   5 Feb 1650
> Apprenticed to John Allardes, 4 years and 1 year (Whitsunday 1648)

Shand, Alexander   31 Oct 1673
> Brother to James Shand, cooper, apprenticed to the said James, 5 years and 1 year

Shand, James   7 Apr 1662
> Son to the late Robert Shand in Asshallach, apprenticed to William Glenny, cooper, 6 years

Sheriff, William   30 Apr 1635
> Second son of Alexander Sheriff in Colhay, to John Webster, merchant, for 5 years

Shirrar, William   29 Aug 1655
> Son in law to William Stewart in Auchlunies, apprenticed to George Adam, weaver, 5 years and 1 year from 26 Nov 1654

Shreff, John   20 Dec 1643
> Son to James Shreff in Easter Forbes with consent of his father, apprenticed to Patrick Chrystie, burgess, 5 years

Sim, Andrew   16 Feb 1648
> Apprenticed to John Maleis, cooper, 6 years and 2 years

Simpson, Alexander   25 Mar 1674
> Son to late Alexander Simpson in Horscruik, apprenticed to James Schand, cooper, 5 years and 1 year

Simpson, Arthur   1 Dec 1671
    Lawfull son to James Simpson in Ardo, apprenticed to George
    Robertson, shoemaker in Spittell, 4 years and 1 year from 13 Oct
    1668
Simpson, John   16 Jul 1656
    Lawful son to Alexander Simpson in Balmuir, apprenticed to William
    Gordon, tailor, 5 years and 1 year from Whitsunday 1655
Simpson, Thomas   7 Jul 1665
    Lawful son to John Simpson in Tours, apprenticed to William Gordon,
    tailor, 6 years
Simson, William   18 Dec 1649
    Son to William Simson in Collistoun, apprenticed to Samuel Hunter,
    cooper, 5 years and 1 year
Skein, Andrew   29 Apr 1643
    Son to late Robert Skein, glazier, with consent of John Forbes, elder,
    and Gilbert Skein, burgesses his curators, apprenticed to George
    Farquhar, merchant, 5 years and 1 year from Whitsunday,1642
Skene, Patrick   29 Sep 1641
    Son to late James Skene sometime resident in the kirktoun of Nig,
    apprenticed to Robert Beastoun, master of the correction house
    within the burgh, 6 years and 1 year
Sklait, Thomas   2 Oct 1646
    Son to Walter Sklait in Crabstoun, apprenticed to John Hay, weaver,
    6 years and 1 year from 18 Nov 1645
Small, Alexander   8 Jun 1648
    Apprenticed to William Smith, tailor, 7 years and 1 year
Smith, Adam   24 Sep 1660
    Son to William Smith in Dilspro, apprenticed to James Robertson,
    burgess of Aberdeen, 5 years from Whitsunday 1656
Smith, Alexander   1 May 1657
    Son to Arthur Smith in Roray, apprenticed to Robert Burnet,
    merchant, 6 years from 3 Aug 1656
Smith, Alexander   2 Dec 1679
    Son to William Smith at the milne of Gourdas, apprenticed to
    William Gerard, burgess, 5 years
Smith, George   5 Feb 1650
    Apprenticed to William Anderson, cooper, 4 years and 1 year
    (Whitsunday, 1649)
Smith, James   1 May 1655
    Son to Alexander Smith in Kemnay, apprenticed to George Smith,
    tailor, 8 years and 1 year

Aberdeen Apprenticeships

Smith, James   19 Dec 1671
 Eldest son to the late Andrew Smith sometime at Heughheid of
 Finzeans, apprenticed to James Blenshell, weaver, 5 years
Smith, John   31 Dec 1636
 Son to Patrick Smith in Towie, to James Chrystie, tailor, for 5 years
 and 1 year
Smith, John   18 Oct 1648
 Apprenticed to John Ritchie, cooper, 5 years
Smith, Patrick   18 Feb 1659
 Son to the late Robert Smith elder, burgess of Aberdeen,
  apprenticed to Alexander Charles, wright, 2 years and 1 year
Smith, Thomas   31 Mar 1647
 Son to John Smith, apprenticed to Peter Shirres, shoemaker, 5 years
 and 1 year from 11 Nov 1646
Smollett, William   2 Feb 1640
 Son to late Gilbert Smollett, salmon fisher in Aberdeen, to
 Alexander Gordon, weaver, for 7 years and 1 year
Spark, John   6 Feb 1630
 To William Smith, weaver for 6 years and 1 year
Spence, John   19 Nov 1646
 Apprenticed to John Blinshell, weaver, 7 years and 1 year
Stanchall, George   30 Nov 1641
 Apprenticed to Robert Beistoun, master of the Correction House, 5
 years and 1 year
Sterlin, Alexander   23 Jul 1656
 Son to James Sterlin, farmer in Aberdeen, apprenticed to Alexander
  Willox, carpenter, 5 years and 1 year
Steven, William   5 Feb 1650
 Apprenticed to Patrick Gray, wright, 5 years and 1 year, from
 Whitsunday 1646
Steven, William   26 April 1656
 Brother son to William Steven in Hatton of Fintray, apprenticed to
 John Super, merchant, 4 years and 1 year
Stevenson, James   12 Dec 1662
 Son to James Stevenson, shoemaker in Aberdeen, apprenticed to John
 Strachan, weaver, 7 years and 1 year
Stewart, George   19 Nov 1684
 Son to Walter Stewart of Outlaw, apprenticed to John Innes,
 merchant, 4 years
Stiven, George   25 Mar 1674
 Son to William Stivin, farmer in Aberdeen, apprenticed to Gilbert
 Taylor, 5 years and 1 year

Stories, John   11 Apr 1632
    Son to late Andrew Stories, resident in Aberdeen, to William
    Anderson, tailor, 6 years and 1 year
Strachan, Cornelius   25 Jul 1649
    Son to late James Strachan, sometime salmon fisher in Aberdeen,
    apprenticed to William Sangster, younger, weaver, 5 years "as thrall
    and bund printeis, and 2 years for meat and fie"
Strachan, Robert   17 Feb 1670
    Son to late William Strachan in Gilcomstoun, apprenticed to William
    Strachan, smith, 5 years from January 1669
Strathan, Patrick   1 Jul 1643
    Grandson to the late Andrew Makie, burgess, apprenticed to George
    Ross, merchant, 5 years and 1 year
Straquhin, John   1 Mar 1628
    Son to John Straquhin in Pitphichie to Patrick Straquhin, tailor, 5
    years and 1 year
Straquhyn, John   3 Jan 1628
    Son to late John Straquhyn fisher, apprenticed by the kirk-session to
    Robert Walker, weaver, for 6 years and 1 year
Straquhane, Robert   25 Nov 1655
    Son to the late Andrew Straquhane, shoemaker, apprenticed to John
    Peirie, cooper, 5 years
Strath, Alexander   6 Jan 1644
    Son to late William Strath sometime in Petblain, apprenticed to
    George Farquhar, shoemaker, 7 years
Super, John   1 Apr 1647
    Only son to William Super in Brathinsch, apprenticed to Andrew
    Guidaill, burgess, 6 years
Sutherland, Patrick   1 May 1657
    Son to Janet Willox in Aberdeen, apprenticed to John Adame, weaver,
    7 years and 1 year from 10 Mar 1656
Sutor, Alexander   4 Mar 1648
    Son to John Sutor, seivewright, apprenticed to William Henderson,
    weaver, 5 years and 1 year
Sym, George   31 Jul 1667
    Son to John Sym in Cowstains of Fintray, apprenticed to Andrew
    Sym, cooper, 6 years and 1 year
Sym, Patrick   18 Jul 1655
    Son to George Sym in Tarves, apprenticed to Thomas Blinshell,
    weaver, 6 years and 1 year from 19 May 1654
Sym, James   28 Jun 1655
    Son to John Sym at the old milne of Fintray, apprenticed to Thomas
    Smith, shoemaker, 5 years

Symmer, John   30 Nov 1665
    Son to George Symmer in Grandhame, apprenticed to George Scott,
    wright, 5 years and 1 year
Symson, John   26 Oct 1633
    Son to David Symson in Cowlie, apprenticed to William Ord, wright,
    for 5 years and 1 year

T

Tailzeor, Magnus   16 Jun 1648
    Son to late Patrick Tailzeor, apprenticed to William Chessor, tailor,
    6 years and 1 year
Tailzeor, James   5 May 1647
    Son to the late Patrick Tailzeor, mason, sometime in the Burne of
    Cultir, apprenticed to John Henrie, 6 years and 1 year
Tailzeor, John   5 May 1647
    Son to late Patrick Tailzeor, mason, sometime in the Burne of Cultir,
    apprenticed to George Farquhar, shoemaker, 6 years and 1 year
Taylor, Hugh   12 Feb 1672
    Son to James Taylor, apprenticed to Alexander Charles, wright, 6
    years and 1 year from 19 Oct 1671
Taylor, James   26 Feb 1649
    Son to Robert Taylor, wright in Inverurie, apprenticed to Alexander
    Willox, wright, 5 years from 1 Jan 1649
Taylor, James   5 Sep 1649
    Son to late Patrick Taylor, mason, sometime at the Bairne of Culter,
    apprenticed to John Hendrie, shoemaker, 6 years and 1 year (23 Apr
    1647)
Tellie, Alexander   2 Jul 1675
    Son to John Tellie, salmon fisherman, apprenticed to Alexander
    Cragmyll, cooper, 6 years and 1 year from Candlemass 1674
Thomson, Alexander   18 Feb 1652
    Brother german to William Thomson, cooper, apprenticed to the said
    William, 4 years and 1 year, from Whitsunday 1648
Thomson, Francis   12 May 1656
    Lawful son to the late Mr Francis Thomson minister at Peterculter,
    apprenticed to John Gordon, merchant burgess, 4 years and 1 year
Thomson, George   19 Jun 1643
    Brother to Alexander Thomson, advocate in Aberdeen, with consent
    of the said Alexander, apprenticed to George Watt, tailor, 5 years
    and 1 year

Aberdeen Apprenticeships

Thomson, Gilbert   29 Apr 1643
> Apprenticed to Alexander Farquhar, merchant, 5 years from
> Whitsunday, 1642

Thomson, James   6 Oct 1648
> Son to Andrew Thomson in Kirktoun of Rayn, apprenticed to Patrick
> Mackie, burgess, 5 years and 1 year

Thomson, John   14 May 1630
> To Robert Melvill, bookbinder, for 6 years and 1 year

Thomson, John   20 Jan 1647
> Son to the late Alexander Thomson, mariner in Aberdeen, apprenticed
> to John Forbes yr, burgess, 5 years and 1 year

Thomson, William   24 Oct 1639
> Son to John Thomson, Knockhall, apprenticed to James Straquhin,
> cooper, 5 years and 1 year

Thomson, William   17 Feb 1649
> Son to Thomas Thomson in Rain, apprenticed to George Cullen,
> baillie, 4 years from Whitsunday 1648

Tilliry, John   5 Nov 1650
> Son to William Tilliry in Nether Birnes, apprenticed to Andrew
> Horne, 6 years and 1 year

Toshe, James   8 Sep 1641
> Son to John Toshe in the Bray of Kildryme, apprenticed to John
> Warrak, weaver, 5 years after Martinmas 1641

Touch, George   1 Aug 1663
> Son to Alexander Touch, farmer, apprenticed to William Strachan,
> smith in Hardgate, 4 years and 1 year - indenture 9 Jan 1662

Troup, Alexander   5 Jul 1672
> Son to Alexander Troup, saddler, apprenticed to William Peirie,
> merchant, 4 years from 20 Jan 1670

Troup, Alexander   21 Jun 1682
> Son to William Troup in Kinkorth, apprenticed to John Webster,
> merchant, 6 years from Whitsunday 1681

Turner, John   10 Jul 1658
> Son to John Turner in Kirktoun of Birss, apprenticed to Patrick
> Chrystie, merchant, 6 years

Tytler, Patrick   5 May 1637
> Son to Alexander Tytler at the mill of Comars, parish of Kinarny,
> apprenticed to Alexander Ettershank, cooper, 5 years and 1 year

Aberdeen Apprenticeships

U

Udny, Robert   24 Sep 1657
> Lawful son to John Udny of Balbithine, apprenticed to Patrick Moir, late ballie, 6 years from 4 Dec 1657 (*sic*) 1656

Urquhart, Thomas   16 Apr 1661
> Son to Patrick Urquhart in Coldwalls, apprenticed to John Middletoun, tailor, 5 years and 1 year

Urrie, Patrick   15 Jan 1631
> Son to late George Urrie in Noram to George Farquhar, shoemaker, for 5 years and 1 year

W

Walker, Alexander   27 May 1659
> Son to the late William Walker at the Mill of Pottertoune, apprenticed to John Mellis, cooper, 5 years and 2 years

Walker, Andrew   15 May 1641
> Son to David Walker in Auchmull, apprentice to Robert Walker, weaver, 6 years and 1 year

Walker, James   30 Apr 1669
> Son to James Walker, salmon fisher, apprenticed to George Adam, weaver, 5 years and 1 year - indenture 10 Oct 1664

Walker, John   2 Oct 1646
> Eldest son to James Walker at the milne of Kincorth, apprenticed to James Maleis, weaver, 6 years and 1 year from 17 Jan 1646

Walker, Robert   9 Jan 1649
> Apprenticed to William Gray, weaver, 8 years and 1 year

Walker, William   15 May 1666
> Son to John Walker, weaver burgess, apprenticed to William Sangster yr, weaver, 7 years and 1 year from 9 Sept 1665

Watson, Alexander   5 Oct 1646
> Son to Andrew Watson in Auchlie, apprenticed to Gilbert Watson, merchant, 4 years and 1 year from 12 Sep 1646

Watson, George   26 Feb 1642
> Son to William Watson in Todlaw, apprentice to John Edward, weaver, 5 years and 1 year

Watson, James   12 Apr 1636
> Son to Alexander Watson in bakhill of Gourdes, within the parish of Fyvie, to Adam Watson, merchant, for 5 years

Aberdeen Apprenticeships

Watson, William   27 Mar 1660
> Son to John Watson at the Mill of Minnes, apprenticed to Alexander Cruikshank, cooper, 2 years and 1 year

Watt, Patrick   3 Mar 1632
> Son to Adam Watt at the Milne of Auquhorties, to Gilbert Adam, shoemaker, for 5 years and 1 year

Webster, John   28 Jul 1663
> Son to John Webster in Newbait, apprenticed to William Thomson, cooper, 6 years and 1 year - indenture dated 18 Dec 1659

Weir, John   29 Sep 1670
> Lawful son to William Weir, merchant in Elgin, apprenticed to William Gray, merchant, 5 years and 1 year from 11 Sep 1669

Whyte, William   10 Oct 1631
> Son of the late Alexander Whyte, weaver, to George Angus, weaver, for 6 years and 1 year

Williamson, Alexander   15 Mar 1655
> Lawful son to Alexander Williamson in Esslemount, apprenticed to Patrick Moir, baillie of Aberdeen, 6 years and 1 year

Willox, George   20 Feb 1679
> Son to Mr James Willox minister at Kemnay, apprenticed to George Willox elder, merchant, 5 years

Willox, Hugh   6 Nov 1650
> Son to Alexander Willox, wright, apprenticed to Gilbert Malcolm, weaver, 5 years and 1 year

Wilson, Patrick   2 Aug 1648
> Son to Patrick Wilson, resident in Aberdeen, apprenticed to William Sangster, weaver, 5 years and 1 year

Wilson, Robert   27 Oct 1638
> Shoemaker son to David Wilson in Glashemoir, apprenticed to Robert Boyd, shoemaker, 5 years and 1 year

Wishart, Thomas   5 Feb 1650
> Apprenticed to Thomas Mitchell, tailor, 5 years and 1 year

Wood, Patrick   2 Oct 1646
> Son to George Wood, apprenticed to Alexander Norvell, weaver, 6 years and 1 year from 11 Nov 1645

Wylie, William   30 Nov 1663
> Son to James Wyllie in Cuntlahills within the parish of Fetteresso, apprenticed to Robert Moir, dyer, 5 years and 1 year

Aberdeen Apprenticeships

Y

Young, Alexander   5 Jan 1638
> Son to Patrick Young, farmer in Aberdeen, to William Forbes elder, burgess, for 5 years

Young, Alexander   16 Dec 1653
> Son to William Young in Culter Cullen, apprenticed to John Hendry elder, shoemaker, 4 years and 1 year

Young, James   Nov 1663
> Son to James Young in Auchlunes, apprenticed to Alexander Gray, weaver, 5 years and 1 year

Youngson, William   27 May 1647
> Son to Andrew Youngson, resident of Old Aberdeen, apprenticed to Patrick Moir, merchant, 7 years - discharge of apprenticeship given in March 1654

Youngson, William   24 Aug 1654
> Eldest lawful son to Andrew Youngson, resident, apprenticed to Alexander Smith, tailor, 6 years and 1 year from Martinmas 1653

Youngson, William   12 Mar 1659
> Burgess of Aberdeen, apprenticed to Hugh Mackgie, chemist, 5 years from Whitsunday 1658

Yuill, William   21 Sep 1637
> Son to late Thomas Zuill, sometime in Kildrymmie, to John Warrack, weaver, for 5 years

ROLL OF APPRENTICES
BURGH OF ABERDEEN
1700-1750

INTRODUCTION

Economic and social power in medieval and early modern Scottish burghs lay in the hands of a self-perpetuating oligarchy called burgesses. The rights to operate a business and to vote were limited to these burgesses, who, in order to maintain their priviledges, operated what today would be described as a "closed shop". To become a burgess of Aberdeen, one had to be the son of an existing Aberdeen burgess, marry the daughter of a burgess, buy the right, or serve an apprenticeship under a craftsman or merchant in the burgh. For an apprentice who did not qualify on other grounds, it was of paramount importance that his apprenticeship indenture be recorded to ensure that he became entitled in due course to apply to become a burgess.

Although most Royal Burghs maintained a Register of Indentures, very few have been transcribed and subsequently published. This booklet, laid out in alphabetical order, is based on the work of the Victorian antiquarian Alexander M Munro. It is the second in a series of three.

Frances J McDonnell
St Andrews
January 1994

REGISTER OF INDENTURES - BURGH OF ABERDEEN
1701   -   1750

A

Aberdeen, William   10 Jun 1728
> Son to the late Mr Andrew Aberdeen, resident in Old Aberdeen, with
> consent of Mr Alexander Fraser of Powis and Alexander Aberdeen,
> merchant in Old Aberdeen, his curators, apprenticed to George
> Maitland, merchant in Aberdeen, 3 years from Martinmas 1727 - fee
> £20 Stg

Adie, Alexander   15 Jan 1720
> Son to Alexander Adie, farmer in Skeen, apprenticed to William
> Stevenson, weaver, 4 years and 1 year from 15 May 1715 - fee £20
> Scots

Alexander, William   8 Jan 1713
> Second lawful son to the late Mr Walter Alexander late minister at
> Echt, with consent of Mr Alexander Gray minister of the Gospel at
> Foote and Jannet Scot, relict of the said Mr Walter Alexander,
> apprenticed to John Carnegie, dyer, 6 years from 12 Mar 1707.

Allan, Colin   1 Feb 1737
> Son to John Allan, farmer in Mastrick, apprenticed to George Cooper,
> goldsmith, 6 years and 1 year from Nov 1736 - George Cooper
> maintains his apprentice in bed, board and clothing - no fee.

Allan, William   28 Jun 1744
> Son to George Allan, farmer in Mains of Auchingoul, apprenticed to
> John Mearns, watchmaker, 6 years from 18 Jul 1740 - no fee.

Anderson, James   9 Mar 1709
> In Kincardine, apprenticed to Alexander Green, wright, 4 years from
> Martinmas 1705.

Anderson, James   6 Mar 1724
> Son to James Anderson, merchant, with the special advice and
> consent of Isobell Cruickshank, his mother, apprenticed to James
> Anderson, glazier, 7 years from 8 Apr 1720.

Anderson, John   9 Oct 1733
> Son to the late James Anderson in the Hardgate of Aberdeen,
> apprenticed to William Robertson, weaver, 6 years from Martinmas
> 1727 - no fee.

Anderson, Thomas   23 Aug 1710
> Son to George Anderson, farmer in Aberdeen, apprenticed to John
> Adam, weaver, 5 years from Whitsunday 1705.

Angus, Alexander   13 Nov 1710
    Lawful son to Robert Angus in Woodside in Echt parish, apprenticed
    to John Adam, weaver, 7 years and 1 year, from Martinmas 1704.
Angus, John   13 Nov 1710
    Son to Robert Angus in Woodside in Echt parish, apprentice to John
    Adam, weaver, 6 years and 1 year from 27 Nov 1702.

B

Barron, Patrick   10 Jan 1721
    Apprenticed to Patrick Gray, wright, 5 years from 31 May 1717.
Barron, William   15 Jun 1747
    Son to George Barron in Glen of Dyce, apprenticed to Alexander
    Kellie, baker, 5 years and 1 year after 8 Jun 1741 - fee 110 merks.
Bartlet, James   2 Mar 1730
    Son to George Bartlet in Rubislaw, apprenticed to Adam Baxter,
    cooper, 3 1/2 years, being the unexpired period of the indenture
    between James Bartlet and the late James Shand, cooper, dated 10
    Jun 1727 - fee 50 merks.
Bartlet, John   15 Dec 1721
    Lawful son to George Bartlet in Shetockslay, aprenticed to Alexander
    Hill younger, tailor burgess, 5 years and 1 year from Martinmas
    1716.
Baxter, Adam   12 Feb 1723
    Son to Robert Baxter, farmer in Balmilly, apprenticed to James
    Shand, cooper, 6 years and 1 year from 18 Jan 1717 - fee 50 merks.
Birse, James   8 Mar 1733
    Son to William Birse in Kincardine, apprenticed to Thomas Niven,
    merchant, 5 years from Whitsunday 1729 - no fee.
Bonner, Alexander   1 Dec 1730
    Son to William Bonner at Bridge of Dee, apprenticed to Alexander
    Walker, weaver, 5 years from 27 Dec 1726 - no fee.
Braik, William   29 Sep 1726
    Son to William Braik, gardener, apprenticed to Robert Lamb, weaver,
    7 years and 1 year from 5 Oct 1718 - fee £8 Scots.
Brown, John   20 Sep 1744
    Son to John Brown in Kemnay, apprenticed to Robert Joyner, tailor, 6
    years after 1 Apr 1741 - no fee.
Burnet, Charles   22 Feb 1717
    Lawful son to Andrew Burnet in Kinmundy, apprenticed to James
    Jaffray, merchant, 2 years and 1 year in the option of his master,
    from 17 Mar 1715.

Burnet, Charles   28 Jun 1731
> Son to the late John Burnet in Inch, apprenticed to Alexander
> Davidson, cooper, 6 years from Martinmas 1729 - fee £6. 6s Stg, and
> a bedding of clothes or a guinea therefor.

Burnet, Thomas   1 Jul 1732
> Son to Mr Roderick Burnet, late minister of Newhills, with consent
> of Janet and Elizabeth, his sisters and curators, apprenticed to Dr
> James Gregorys elder and younger, physicians, 3 or 4 years in his
> master's option from Whitsun 1731 - fee 300 merks.

C

Cassie, William   9 Feb 1730
> Son to John Cassie, wright, apprenticed to Patrick Barron, wright, 5
> years from 1 Jan 1730.   Indenture signed at Aberdeen and
> Nethermill of Cruden.   Cautioners, the father and William Moir of
> Whitehill - fee £3 Stg.

Catto, Alexander   1 Jan 1726
> Son to William Catto, farmer in Aberdeen, apprenticed to James
> Davidson, weaver, 6 years and 1 year from 10 Jun 1720 - fee £8
> Scots.

Chalmers, Alexander   1 Dec 1726
> Son to the late James Chalmers, maltman, with consent of Isobell
> Lumsden, his mother, apprenticed to George Leonard, tailor, 5 years
> from 20 Mar 1722 - fee 50 merks.

Chalmers, James   16 Mar 1733
> Son to Peter Chalmers, resident in Aberdeen, apprenticed to Thomas
> Murray, tailor, 6 years and 1 year from Lammas 1729 - no fee;
> cautioner Mr James Chalmers, Student in Divinity.

Chalmers, Lewis   14 Aug 1738
> Son to Mr James Chalmers, Professor of Divinity at the Marischal
> College, apprenticed to George Cooper, goldsmith, 6 years and 1 year
> after Martinmas next - no fee, his father to furnish during 6 years
> all necessary wearing apparel and keep in diet.

Chalmers, William   15 Dec 1719
> Lawful son to George Chalmers, MA, in Aberdeen, apprenticed to
> Gilbert Moir, cooper, 6 years from 20 Oct 1713 - fee £40 Scots.

Chalmers, William   8 Nov 1731
> Son to James Chalmers, merchant, apprenticed to John Sim, cooper,
> 6 years from 1 Dec 1730 - fee £4 Stg.

Cheyne, Alexander   29 Sep 1726
    Son to John Cheyne, quarrier, apprenticed to Charles Still, weaver, 6
    years and 1 year from 17 Aug 1726 - fee £8 Scots.

Clerihew, John   22 Jul 1736
    Son to John Clerihew, resident in Aberdeen, apprenticed to William
    Harthill, shoemaker, 6 years from 1 Aug - fee £20 Scots.

Clerk, Alexander   1 May 1733
    Son to Alexander Clerk in Bogmiln, apprenticed to Francis Morison,
    wright, 5 years from Whitsunday 1731 - no fee.

Clerk, William   9 Oct 1733
    Son to John Clerk in Bridgend of Arbuthnott, apprenticed to Robert
    Lamb, weaver, 5 years from 1 Apr 1731 - no fee.

Cooper, John   1 Apr 1727
    Son to Alexander Cooper in Maryculter parish, apprenticed to
    Alexander Elmsly, shoemaker, 5 years from 15 Mar 1727 - fee £40
    Scots.   John Taylor, writer in Aberdeen, cautioner.

Cowts, James   10 Jan 1721
    Lawful son to the late William Cowts, weaver in Glenmuik,
    apprenticed to Alexander Lichton, weaver, 8 years from Martinmas
    1719 - fee 20 merks with two pair of blankets.

Craig, William   14 May 1743
    Son to George Craig in Rarchel, in the parish of Fetteresso,
    apprenticed to John Sim, cooper, 6 years from 2 Jul 1742 - fee £5
    Stg.

Cromar, Thomas   1 May 1729
    Son to the late Thomas Cromar, salmon fisher, apprenticed to
    Alexander Smith, shoemaker, with consent of Barbara Moir, widow of
    the said Thomas Cromar, 7 years from Martinmas 1723 - no fee.

Cruickshank, Robert   6 May 1727
    Son to Patrick Cruickshank, tailor, apprenticed to William Robertson
    younger, weaver, 6 years and 1 year from 1 Jun 1720 - fee 20 merks.

Cruickshank, William   6 Mar 1724
    Son to Alelxander Cruickshank, wright in Aberdeen, apprenticed to
    William Davidson, weaver, 7 years from Whitsunday 1717.

Cruikshank, Francis   2 Feb 1732
    Son to Robert Cruikshank, silversmith in Old Aberdeen, apprenticed
    to George Cooper, goldsmith, 6 years, from Martinmas 1731 - no fee.

Cruikshank, James   10 May 1734
    Son to George Cruikshank, farmer at Greentree, apprenticed to
    William Stivenson, weaver, 7 years from Martinmas 1727 - no fee.

Cruikshank, John   20 Sep 1731
    Son to Patrick Cruikshank, tailor, apprenticed to William Cruikshank,
    weaver, 5 years from Martinmas 1726 - no fee.

Cuming, James   31 Dec 1717
    Lawful son to James Cuming in Kirkhill of Nig, apprenticed to Gilbert
    Duff, cooper, 6 years and 1 year from 1 Mar 1711.
Cumming, James   23 Dec 1738
    Son to the late John Cumming of Kininmont, with consent of Mary
    Keith, his mother, and the new deceased George Keith, advocate in
    Aberdeen, apprenticed to Thomas Paul, merchant, 4 years after Aug
    1735 - fee 700 merks, with 50 merks for a bedding of cloth.   Paul
    to find his apprentice in bed, board and washing, and before expiry of
    apprenticeship to send him to Holland or any other foreign country as
    he should have occasion for going about his master's affairs there.

D

Dallas, James   30 Jul 1741
    Son to Andrew Dallas, wright, apprenticed to William Bennet,
    saddler, 5 years from Whitsunday last - fee £100 Scots.
Davidson, Alexander   12 Feb 1723
    Son to George Davidson at Gerriesburn, apprenticed to Robert
    Davidson, cooper, 6 years after Whitsunday 1723 - fee £60 Scots.
Davidson, James   6 Mar 1724
    Son to James Davidson, farmer in Conland, parish of Forgue,
    apprenticed to Gilbert Duff, cooper, 6 years from 20 Sep 1723 - fee
    £48 Scots.
Davidson, John   2 Mar 1711
    Lawful son to Thomas Davidson in Kirktown of Skeen, apprenticed to
    Robert Morgan, merchant, 5 years from Martinmas 1706.
Davidson, John   4 May 1737
    Son to the late George Davidson, shoemaker, apprenticed to Thomas
    Murray, tailor, with consent of the Kirk Session; 6 years and 1 year
    from 21 Jun 1731 - fee £8 Scots.
Davidson, John   15 Mar 1739
    Son to Thomas Davidson in Craigsley, apprenticed to Alexander
    Mitchell of Colpna, merchant, and one of the present baillies of
    Aberdeen, 6 years, from Whitsunday 1735 - no fee, the father to
    maintain in all necessary garments except shoes, and the master to
    pay £3 Stg for the last year.
Davidson, John   19 Feb 1742
    Son to Alexander Davidson, merchant in Old Meldrum, apprenticed to
    George Cooper, goldsmith, 7 years after Martinmas 1741 - no fee;
    cautioners, his father and William Davidson, ballie of Aberdeen.

Davidson, Robert   1 Jul 1715
    Son to George Davidson of Garriesburn, apprenticed to Gilbert Moir,
    cooper, 6 years and 1 year from 13 May 1709.
Davidson, Robert   25 Jun 1728
    Apprenticed to Abraham Davidson, merchant in Aberdeen, his
    brother, 2 years from 8 Oct 1726 - no fee.   Obligation to send the
    apprentice to London, Holland, or some place beyond seas.
Davidson, William   14 Nov 1713
    Son to Andrew Davidson in Aberdeen, apprenticed to Alexander
    Lichton, burgess, 5 years from Martinmas 1707.
Donald, Alexander   14 Jun 1750
    Son to William Donald, farmer in Aberdeen, apprenticed to Alexander
    Thomson, shoemaker, 7 years from 15 Jun 1743 - no fee.
Donald, James   15 Oct 1707
    Son to Alexander Donald in the parish of Newhills, apprenticed to
    William Donald, baker, 5 years and 1 year from Whitsunday 1704.
Donald, James   2 Nov 1744
    Son to James Donald, merchant in Cairnwhelp, apprenticed to Walter
    Ross, merchant, 4 years from 20 Nov 1740 - no fee.
Donald, Robert   18 Jun 1727
    Son to David Donald in Cutlehill, parish of Newhills, apprenticed to
    Alexander Angus, weaver, 6 years and 1 year from 3 March 1721 - no
    fee.
Donald, Robert   23 May 1750
    Son to Robert Donald, weaver, apprenticed to John Reid, weaver, 6
    years after Whitsunday 1748 - no fee.
Douglas, George   15 Jan 1720
    Lawful son to Robert Douglas of Bridgeford, apprenticed to George
    Maitland, merchant, 3 years from Lammes 1719 - fee 500 merks.
Duguid, William   2 Mar 1711
    Son to William Duguid, miller at Gilcomstoun, apprenticed to
    Alexander Ragg, merchant, 3 years from Whitsunday 1708.
Duncan, John   17 Feb 1732
    Son to Alexander Duncan in Newtoun of Drum, apprenticed to William
    Strachan, dyer, five years from 31 Jul 1728 - fee £50 Scots and
    three bolls meal.
Duncan, Patrick   1 Apr 1727
    Son to the late Alexander Duncan, weaver, with consent of Jean
    Blenshell, his mother, apprenticed to James Simson, tailor, 8 years
    from 18 Feb 1720.   Cautioners, his mother and Robert Lamb, weaver.

E

Ellice, George   12 Feb 1723
    Son to George Ellice in Knockleith, apprenticed to Thomas Nivie,
    merchant, 3 years from Whitsunday 1720 - fee 500 merks.
Elphinston, John   25 Jul 1729
    Son to John Elphinston in Easter Cullairly, apprenticed to Alexander
    Forbes, Lockermick, merchant, 3 years from Martinmas 1726.

F

Farquhar, William   15 Jan 1712
    Son to Mr Robert Farquhar master of the Grammar School of
    Banchory, apprenticed to William Smith, merchant, 3 years from
    Martinmas 1711.
Farquharson, Charles   30 Jul 1728
    Son to Lewis Farquharson in Bog of cromar, apprenticed to George
    Simpson, cooper, 7 years from 31 May - fee £50 Scots, with a
    bedding of clothes at his entry, and two bolls of meal at Martinmas
    1728.
Farquharson, Charles   1 Mar 1733
    Son to Donald Farquharson of Micras, apprenticed to Thomas Niven,
    merchant, 5 years from 10 Jun 1730 - fee 400 merks.
Farquharson, Francis   17 Sep 1734
    Son to the late Francis Farquharson of Shiels, with consent of Harry
    Farquharson, his brother, apprenticed to George Garioch, saddler, 5
    years, from 1 Sep 1733 - fee £20 Stg.
Farquharson, George   16 Mar 1733
    Son to Donald Farquharson in Hattoun of Skeen, apprenticed to John
    Sim, cooper, 6 years from Feb 1733 - fee £5 Stg and a bedding of
    clothes; cautioners the father and Charles Farquharson in Lairshill.
Farquharson, James   29 Sep 1726
    Son to the late Harry Farquharson of Whitehouse, with consent of
    Francis Farquharson of Whitehouse, his brother, apprenticed to
    James Ferguson, cooper, 6 years and 1 year from 19 May 1724 - fee
    £72 Scots with two bolls of meal.
Ferguson, Alexander   3 May 1714
    Lawful son to Alexander Ferguson, farmer in Drumside in Balhelvie
    parish, apprenticed to James Ferguson, cooper, 6 years and 1 year
    from 22 May 1713.

Forbes, Alexander   19 Apr 1740
   Son to Magnus Forbes in Nether Loirstoun, in the parish of Nigg, apprenticed to William Strachan, weaver, 6 1/2 years from 9 Jun 1739 - no fee.

Forbes, George   16 Mar 1733
   Son to George Forbes of Bellabeg, apprenticed to Robert Chalmers, cooper, 6 years from Whitsunday 1729 - fee 100 merks.

Forbes, Hugh   1 Jul 1732
   Son to William Forbes of Belnaboddach, apprenticed to Gilbert Duff, cooper, 7 years - fee £6 Stg with a bedding of clothes.

Forbes, James   27 Nov 1744
   Son to William Forbes in Miln of Collithie, apprenticed to Alexander Davidson, cooper, 6 years after 1 Jul 1740 - fee £100 Scots.

Forbes, John   4 Dec 1736
   Son to George Forbes of Alfoord, apprenticed to William Midleton, merchant, 3 years from 25 Jun last - fee £600 Scots in three instalments. "Alfoord maintains his son in back cloths and other necessary apparel and in case he get a horse to ride to markets he likewise to pay the hire to the said William Midleton from time to time."

Forbes, William   14 Oct 1701
   Son to Robert Forbes in Frosterhill, apprenticed to William Simpson, merchant, 4 years from 6 Jan 1701.

Forbes, William   23 May 1750
   Son to the late Alexander Forbes in Aquorthen, apprenticed to Robert Lamb, weaver, 5 years from Whitsunday 1746 - no fee.

Fraser, Alexander   24 Sep 1742
   Son to James Fraser, farmer in Aberdeen, apprenticed to Alexander Thomson, shoemaker, 5 years after Martinmas 1737 - fee £12 Scots and a bedding of clothes.

Fraser, William   2 Mar 1711
   Son to the late Andrew Fraser in Cullarly, apprenticed to James Hay, barber and periwigg maker, 3 years from Martinmas 1706.

G

Gammack, Alexander   22 Apr 1740
   Son to the late Alexander Gammack in New Deer, apprenticed to James Abernethy, merchant, 4 years from 15 May 1736 - no fee, the master to pay £24 Scots yearly during apprenticeship.

Garioch, Alexander   4 Nov 1725
    Son to William Garioch of Tilliechettly, apprenticed to Alexander
    Livingston, merchant, 5 years from Whitsunday 1721.
Garioch, Andrew   9 Mar 1709
    Son to the minister of Culsalmond (Rev William Garioch),
    apprenticed to Thomas Orem, merchant, 3 or 4 years in his master's
    option, from 6 Feb 1707.
Gordon, Alexander   17 Jan 1739
    Son to the late George Gordon of Kirkulloch, apprenticed to James
    Smith, saddler, 6 years from 1 Oct 1733 - fee £15 Stg; cautioner,
    Margaret Duff, Lady Glengarrock.
Gordon, George   17 Jan 1738
    Son to George Gordon, weaver at Foveran, apprenticed to William
    Davidson, weaver, 6 years after Martinmas 1731 - no fee.
Gordon, John   9 Dec 1728
    Son to Peter Gordon of Blackhills, apprenticed to Gilbert Duff,
    cooper, 7 years from martinmas 1728 - fee £50 Scots and two bolls
    of meal.

H

Hadden, Alexander   14 May 1743
    Son to William Hadden, weaver, apprenticed to William Brebner,
    merchant, 5 years after Whitsunday 1738 - no fee.
Hadden, John   1 Sep 1748
    Son to William Hadden, weaver, apprenticed to James Norrie, tailor,
    6 years after Whitsunday 1743 - no fee.
Haddin, William   15 Apr 1741
    Son to William Haddin, weaver, apprenticed to Andrew Hutcheon,
    tailor, 6 years from Whitsunday 1738 - no fee.
Hardie, William   12 Feb 1723
    Son to the late James Hardie, sometime Deacon to the Hammermen
    trade, apprenticed to John Fowler, tailor, 5 years and 1 year from 5
    Nov 1717 - fee £24 Scots.
Harrow, John   26 Dec 1737
    Son to William Harrow, workman, apprenticed to Francis Massie,
    piriewigmaker, 6 years from 1 Jan 1732 - no fee.
Harthill, William   21 May 1722
    Lawful son to William Harthill, gardener in Aberdeen, apprenticed to
    Alexander Smith, shoemaker, 5 years and 1 year from 3 Sep 1717.

Harvie, William   15 Dec 1719
    Lawful son to William Harvie in Seaton, apprenticed to Gilbert Moir,
    cooper, 6 years and 1 year from 9 Jul 1719 - fee £48 Scots
Hay, William   21 May 1722
    Son to John Hay, resident in Aberdeen, by his cautioner Andrew
    Murray, late Collector of the Kirk Session, apprenticed to James
    Hardie, blacksmith, 8 years, from Candlemas 1711.
Henderson, David   2 May 1728
    Son to William Henderson in Dyce, apprenticed to William Moir,
    cooper, 6 years and 1 year from 23 May 1722 - fee 50 merks Scots.
    Alexander Cooper, music master, cautioner.
Horn, James   9 Mar 1709
    Son to George Horn, horse hirer, apprenticed to James Douglas,
    baker, 6 years..

I

Ingram, John   11 Jul 1739
    Son to William Ingram, resident in Aberdeen, apprenticed to William
    Smith, merchant and late Ballie, 5 years from 1 Mar last - no fee.
Innes, James   15 Sep 1750
    Son to John Innes, silversmith in Huntly, apprenticed to Colin Allan,
    goldsmith, 5 years after 15 May 1749, no fee; Mr John Gordon at
    Robinstoun, cautioner.
Irvine, James   1 Jul 1715
    Lawful son to Robert Irvine of Corniehaugh, apprenticed to Gilbert
    Moir, cooper, 6 years and 1 year from 1 Aug 1708.

J

Jack, George   25 Mar 1749
    Son to alexander Jack in Gask of Cruden, apprenticed to William
    Moir, cooper, 6 years after 1 Jan 1745 - no fee.
Jaffray, John   27 Apr 1734
    Son to Alexander Jaffray, resident in Aberdeen, apprenticed to
    James Robertson, weaver, 6 years and 1 year from Whitsunday 1727
    - fee 20 merks.
Johnston, William   1 Sep 1732
    Son to the late Patrick Johnston, mason, apprenticed to Robert
    Robertson, cardmaker, 5 years from 13 Nov 1727 - fee £2 Stg.

Jop, Alexander   3 Jul 1738
    Son to James Jop, merchant in Huntly, apprenticed to George Wright, cooper, 6 years after 16 May last - fee £5 10s Stg, with sufficient bedding of clothes.

K

Keith, Thomas   3 Jan 1743
    Son to the late Mr Thomas Keith in Tilburies, apprenticed to George Wright, cooper 7 years after 1 Jan 1743 - fee £50 Scots; cautioners James Keith in Tulburies and John Wilson, workman.

Kellie, George   1 Dec 1726
    Son to William Kellie, maltster, apprenticed to George Spence, cooper, 6 years from 1 Apr 1726 - fee 100 merks.

Kilgour, John   4 Nov 1713
    Second lawful son to the late Thomas Kilgour, sometime watchmaker in the burgh of Inverness, with consent of William McLean, goldsmith, the curator nominated by his said father, apprenticed to Andrew Jaffrey, merchant, 5 years from Apr 1711.

Knowes, George   9 Mar 1709
    Lawful son to James Knowes in Portlethan, apprenticed to James Pratt, tailor, 5 years from Lammas 1705.

L

Lamb, William   2 May 1737
    Son to James Lamb in Kirktoun of Fetteresso, apprenticed to Robert Lamb, weaver, 5 years from Whitsunday 1733 - no fee.

Largue, James   1 Mar 1726
    Son to Patrick Largue in Drumdollo, apprenticed to Gilbert Duff, cooper, 6 years from Candlemas 1726 - fee £52 Scots. Alexander Largue in Drumdollo, brother german to the said James, cautioner.

Legertwood, John   13 Dec 1736
    Son to the late Mr Alexander Legertwood, resident in Aberdeen, and Margaret Ferrier, his spouse, apprenticed to William Chrystie, merchant in Aberdeen, 5 years after Whitsunday 1736 - fee 100 merks Scots.

Lendrum, William   1 Apr 1743
    Son to William Lendrum in Watrichmoor, apprenticed to Alexander Thomson, shoemaker, 3 years after Whitsunday next - fee £74 Scots.

Leslie, Gilbert   24 Oct 1710
    Son to the late Gilbert Leslie, shoemaker, apprenticed to John Craig,
    baker, 6 years from Candlemas 1710.
Lewis, William   5 Jun 1733
    Son to the late Caleb Lewis, resident in Aberdeen, apprenticed to
    George Wright, cooper, 6 years - fee £69 13s 4d Scots and a bedding
    of clothes; cautioner George Smith in Broomend.
Ligertwood, James   16 May 1746
    Son to the late Alexander Ligertwood, sometime resident in
    Aberdeen, apprenticed to William Young, merchant, 4 years after 1
    May 1742 - fee 300 merks.   Margaret Ferrier, his mother, consents
    and Mr John Gelly, minister at Nigg, cautioner.
Livingston, Andrew   2 Mar 1711
    Son to Mr Andrew Livingston minister at Kigg, apprenticed to
    William Cruickshank, merchant, 4 years, from Whitsunday 1709.

                               M

Main, Alexander   29 Apr 1737
    Son to George Main in Portlethen, apprenticed to George Main,
    shoemaker, 5 years from 13 Jul 1736 - no fee.
Man, William   24 Oct 1738
    Son to the late James Man at Miln of Aden, with consent of Jean
    Clerk, his mother, apprenticed to Thomas Glenny, merchant, 2 years
    from 12 Jan 1737 - fee £10 Stg, his mother to aliment and maintain
    him in diet, washing and clothing.
Mar, John   23 Sep 1734
    Son to Alexander Mar, shoemaker, apprenticed to James Leonard,
    barber, 4 years from 30 Dec 1730 - fee £30 Scots.
Massie, Francis   15 Oct 1707
    Lawful son to the late George Massie sometime in Norham,
    apprenticed to Robert Murray, barber, 3 years from 9 Jan 1706.
Mathieson, Andrew   18 Jun 1727
    Son to James Mathieson, weaver, apprenticed to William Hadden,
    weaver, 5 years from Whitsunday 1722.
McIndowe, Charles   1 Jul 1740
    Son to Charles McIndowe, resident, apprenticed to William Moir,
    cooper, 7 years after 4 Jul 1733 - fee £5 Stg.
McKenzie, Alexander   27 Oct 1727
    Son to David McKenzie, sometime in Miln of Kinaldie, with consent of
    John Strachan, merchant in Edinburgh, apprenticed to William
    Duncan, baker, 5 years from 1 May 1723 - no fee.

McDonald, Alexander   2 May 1728

Son to the late Duncan McDonald, farmer in Killeyn parish, apprenticed to Thomas Niven, merchant, 4 years - no fee.   Mr Alexander keith, minister at Cruden, cautioner.

Mercer, Alexander   1 Dec 1726

Son to John Mercer elder, salmon fisher, apprenticed to George Spence, cooper, 7 years from 1 Jul 1723 - fee £48 Scots. Cautioners, his father and James Milne, barber.

Meston, James   20 Sep 1744

Son to James Meston, resident, apprenticed to David Moncrief, baker, 7 years after Whitsunday 1743 - no fee.

Midleton, John   6 Aug 1736

Son to the late John Midleton, farmer in Ferryhill, apprenticed to Francis Massie, barber, 7 years from 3 Feb 1736 - no fee, only a bedding of clothes.

Moir, Alexander   29 Jan 1747

Son to the late Alexander Moir, tailor in Old Aberdeen, apprenticed to James Birnie jr, shoemaker, 5 years after Whitsunday 1742 - fee £20 Scots and a bedding of clothes; cautioners Agnes Booth, his mother, and William Booth, sailor.

Moir, Gilbert   23 Sep 1734

Son to James Moir, maltster, apprenticed to George Cooper, goldsmith, 7 years from 23 Mar 1734 - no fee; James Moir to aliment his son in bed, board and washing.

Moreson, Francis   31 Dec 1717

Lawful son to the late Alexander Moreson at Pennyburne in the parish of Forgue, apprenticed to Robert Law, wright, for the time unexpired in the indenture between the late George Massie, wright, and the said Francis, dated May 1715.

Morgan, George   8 Jul 1738

Son to Robert Morgan, stabler, apprenticed to William Stevenson yr, weaver, 6 years from Lammas 1734 - no fee, his father to maintain him in all necessary wearing apparel.

Morgan, John   1 May 1736

Son to Peter Morgan in Bogfairnie, apprenticed to James Ferguson, cooper, 6 years and 1 year from 29 Jul 1729 - fee £4 Stg and two bolls of meal.

Murray, Adam   27 Nov 1744

Son to Adam Murray in Reidfold, apprenticed to Robert Aikman, wright, 5 years after Martinmas 1739 - fee £54 Scots.

Murray, George   29 Aug 1728

Son to Angus Murray in the parish of Rogart, apprenticed to William Thomson, tailor, 5 years and 1 year from 29 Aug 1727.   Cautioner,

Murray, George   29 Aug 1728
   Son to Angus Murray in the parish of Rogart, apprenticed to William
   Thomson, tailor, 5 years and 1 year from 29 Aug 1727. Cautioner,
   Mr William Stiven, Doctor of the Grammar School - fee £30 Scots.
Murray, William   1 Apr 1734
   Son to Mr William Murray, minister of the Gospel in Old Aberdeen,
   apprenticed to Thomas Nivie, merchant, 4 years from 10 Apr 1733
   - fee £6 Stg for each year.

N

Naughty, John   27 Jul 1739
   Son to William Naughty, wright, apprenticed to Alexander Duncan,
   barber and piriewig maker, 5 years from 2 Aug 1734 - no fee.

O

Ogilvie, Alexander   20 May 1734
   Late Clerk of the Customes at the Port of Aberdeen, apprenticed to
   James Keith, merchant, 3 years after 23 Feb 1734 - fee 100 merks
   Scots.
Ogilvie, George   25 Oct 1748
   Son to Alexander Ogilvie, Customhouse clerk at Dundee, apprenticed
   to William Proctor, saddler, 7 1/2 years from 15 Nov 1744 - no fee.
Oliver, Ebenezer   5 Jun 1741
   Son to Mr Steven Oliver, minister of the Gospel at Forbes,
   apprenticed to Robert Chalmers, cooper, 6 years from Whitsunday
   1735 - fee 100 merks.

P

Panton, George   1 Feb 1726
   Son to John Panton in Burnside of Udoch, apprenticed to John Sim,
   cooper, 6 years from Whitsunday 1724 - fee £4 Stg, with one
   bedding of cloth, James Ogilvie, Comptroller of his Majesty's
   Customs at the Port of Aberdeen, cautioner for the apprentice fee.
Paul, John   8 Nov 1731
   Son to the late James Paul, merchant, apprenticed to John Sim,
   cooper, 6 years from 29 Apr 1728 - fee £5 Stg; cautioner Thomas
   Paul, merchant.

Philp, William   5 Jun 1733
    Son to the late Thomas Philp, maltman, with consent of James
    Mackie, collector of the Kirk of Session, apprenticed to Robert Lamb,
    weaver, 6 years and 1 year from Martinmas 1726 - fee £8 Scots.
Porter, Patrick   25 Oct 1748
    Son to John Procter (Porter?) in Clayfurs of Easter Elchies,
    apprenticed to William Proctor, saddler, 6 years after Martinmas
    1742 - no fee.
Proctor, William   30 Sep 1732
    Son to William Proctor in Mains of Achindore, apprenticed to George
    Gairoch, saddler, 6 years from 17 Nov 1730.   Master to pay £3 for
    each of the last three years and maintain the apprentice in bed,
    board and washing.

R

Rammage, Alexander   15 Apr 1740
    Son to Robert Rammage, heelmaker, apprenticed to William Harthill,
    shoemaker, 5 years from 22 Apr 1735 - fee £30 Scots and a
    sufficient bedding of clothes.
Rankin, George   10 Jan 1721
    Son to George Rankine of Auchrynie, apprenticed to William Mowat,
    merchant, 4 or 5 years, at the option of George Rankines, elder and
    younger, from Lammas 1718 - fee 600 merks.
Reid, John   18 Jun 1727
    Son to Thomas Reid, weaver, apprenticed to William Davidson,
    weaver, 7 years and 1 year, from 7 Sept 1719 - fee £8 Scots.
Reid, Robert   10 Jun 1746
    Son to Alexander Reid, tailor at Lonhead, apprenticed to Robert
    Joiner, tailor, 8 years after 21 Jun 1739 - no fee.
Reid, William   17 Jan 1738
    Son to Alexander Reid, tailor in Lonhead, apprenticed to Robert
    Spring, tailor, 5 years and 1 year after 4 May 1732 - fee £8 Scots,
    with a pair of blankets and a cod.
Revell, John   16 Jul l1739
    Son to William Revell, resident, apprenticed to William Stevenson,
    weaver, 5 years from 27 Sep 1738 - no fee.
Ritchie, John   4 Nov 1724
    Son to George Ritchie, stabler, apprenticed to Andrew Grant, weaver,
    5 years from Lammas 1721 - fee £25 Scots.

Robertson, Andrew   8 Dec 1731
    Son to the late Arthur Robertson in Cuperstoun, apprenticed to
    James Cushny, shoemaker, 5 years from 9 Dec 1726 - fee £30 Scots.
    Cautioners, James and Thomas, brothers to the said Andrew and
    George Robertson, goldsmith, for his fidelity and honesty.
Robertson, James   8 Jun 1717
    Son to George Robertson in Bowcraig in the parish of Boyndie,
    apprenticed to Alexander Lyall, shoemaker, 5 years from 7 Aug 1712.
Robertson, James   26 Aug 1730
    Son to the late George Robertson, goldsmith, apprenticed to George
    Cooper, goldsmith, 6 years from Whitsunday 1729.   Cautioner
    Katherine Moir, his mother - no fee, but a bedding of clothes.
Robertson, Patrick   27 Apr 1712
    Lawful son to Patrick Robertson in Rubislaw, apprenticed to
    Alexander Lyall late deacon of the shoemaker trade, 5 years from
    Martinmas 1710.
Robertson, Robert   12 Feb 1723
    Son to Robert Robertson, resident in Aberdeen, apprenticed to
    William Glenny, cardmaker, 4 years and 1 year, from Martinmas 1720
    - fee £48 Scots.
Robertson, William   25 Oct 1748
    Son to William Robertson in Tillidrone, apprenticed to William
    Procter, saddler, 7 years after 27 May 1747 - no fee.

                                    S

Sangster, William   5 Apr 1732
    Son to William Sangster, shoemaker, apprenticed to William
    Harthill, shoemaker, 6 years from 12 Apr 1729 - fee £36 Scots with
    a bedding of clothes.
Shand, James   17 Sep 1710
    Son to the late Robert shand at Kirk of Forgue, apprenticed to Gilbert
    Moir, cooper, 6 years and 1 year, from Candlemas 1704.
Shank, Mathew   8 Oct 1715
    Son to Mr Martin Shank, minister of the Gospel at Banchory,
    apprenticed to William Smith, merchant, 3 years from 22 Sep 1713.
Sharp, John   2 Dec 1706
    Lawful son to Arthur Sharp, gardener, apprenticed to James Hay,
    barber, 4 years from 13 Sep 1700.
Shepherd, William   18 Apr 1732
    Eldest son to William Shepherd yr, in Findon, apprenticed to John
    Mair, merchant, 3 years after Martinmas 1730 - fee £5 Stg.

Short, James   25 Sep 1723
> Son to the late William Short, sometime farmer in Nether Dummay,
> parish of Dumblet, with consent of John Maitland, maltman in
> Aberdeen, apprenticed to James Shand, cooper, 6 years and 1 year
> from 1 Jun 1721 - fee £40 Scots.

Simpson, George   7 Feb 1713
> Lawful son to William Simpson in Craig of Balhelvie, apprenticed to
> William More, cooper, 6 years and 1 year from 19 Feb 1712.

Smith, George   2 Dec 1735
> Son to William Smith, weaver in Old Aberdeen, apprenticed to James
> Robertson yr, weaver, 6 years and 1 year from 1 Jun 1730 - no fee;
> cautioner, James Moir of Stonniewood.

Smith, James   6 Dec 1728
> Son to John Smith, baker, apprenticed to William Stivenson, weaver,
> 5 years from Whitsunday 1724 - no fee.

Smith, James   20 May 1734
> Son to William Smith, schoolmaster in Aberdeen, apprenticed to
> Robert Joyner, tailor, 7 years and 1 year at the option of the master,
> from 13 Aug 1729 - fee £8 Scots as a Session apprentice.

Smith, John   29 Jan 1748
> Son to the late Alexander Smith, shoemaker, apprenticed to William
> Booth, shoemaker, 4 years after 3 Sep 1745 - £40 Scots.

Smith, Robert   29 Apr 1737
> Son to John Smith in Lay, apprenticed to George Robertson,
> shoemaker, 5 years from Jan 1734 - fee £4 Stg.

Smith, William   4 Nov 1725
> Son to Gilbert Smith in Ord, apprenticed to Patrick Gray, wright, 5
> years and 1 year from Martinmas 1719 - fee £56 Scots.

Smith, William   11 Nov 1740
> Son to William Smith in Spithill, apprenticed to James Davidson,
> weaver, 6 years and 1 year from 6 Jan 1734 - no fee.

Spark, William   ? Jan 1731
> Son to Thomas Spark, salmon fisher, apprenticed to Francis Molyson,
> wheelwright, 5 years from Martinmas 1726 - fee £5 Stg; cautioner
> Thomas Mercer.

Spence, Alexander   5 Jun 1733
> Son to Thomas Spence, tailor at the Denburn of Aberdeen,
> apprenticed to George Knows, tailor, 6 years, after Martinmas 1728
> - fee £36 Scots and a bedding of clothes.

Spence, George   22 Apr 1712
> Lawful son to George Spence at Tyrie, apprenticed to Gilbert Duff,
> cooper, 3 years from Whitsunday 1710.

Stalker, George   27 Oct 1727
    Son to James Stalker, resident in Aberdeen, apprenticed to
    Alexander Lichton, weaver, 5 years from Martinmas 1723 - fee 40
    merks Scots and a bedding of cloths.

Stott, Patrick   18 Jun 1727
    Son to Patrick Stott, farmer in Aberdeen, apprenticed to William
    Davidson, weaver, 7 years from Whitsunday 1720.   Cautioner,
    Archibald French, dyer.

Strachan, Andrew   2 Mar 1711
    Lawful son to the late Andrew Strachan Sheriff Clerk of Kincardine,
    apprenticed to William Mowat, merchant, 5 years from Whitsunday,
    1704.   Indenture made with the "special advice and consent of the
    late Mr John Mowat of Balquholly, advocate."

Strachan, William   2 Mar 1711
    Lawful son to John Strachan of Kincardine, apprenticed to George
    French, dyer, 5 years from Whitsunday 1708.

Stuart, John   2 Jul 1736
    Son to the late William Stuart in Kirkhill of Gartlie, apprenticed to
    John sim, cooper, 6 years from 17 Jun - fee £6 Stg.

Stuart, Robert   8 Nov 1740
    Son to the late Robert Stuart, farmer in Aberdeen, apprenticed to
    John Reid, weaver, 5 years from Whitsunday 1737 - no fee.

Sutherland, William   24 Mar 1750
    Son to George Sutherland, workman in Aberdeen, apprenticed to
    William Annand, hooker in Aberdeen, 5 years after Candlemas 1746
    - fee 50 merks.

Symmers, William   25 Sep 1723
    Son to the late Alexander Symmers in Torrie, with consent of George
    Symmers in Torrie, his brother german, apprenticed to James Shand,
    cooper, 6 years from 1 Jun 1722 - fee 100 merks.

T

Thom, James   15 Dec 1719
    Son of the late Gilbert Thom in Hazlehead, apprenticed to Gilbert
    Duff, cooper, with consent of James and Robert Catanachs,
    merchants, 7 years, from 1 Oct 1714 - fee £48 Scots.

Thom, John   21 May 1722
    Lawful son to James Thom, gardener, apprenticed to James Smith,
    blacksmith, 5 years and 1 year, from 13 Nov 1713 - fee 20 merks.

Thom, Robert   20 Feb 1747
> Resident, apprenticed to John Thom, blacksmith, 6 years after 7 Jan 1742 - no fee.

Thomson, Alexander   20 Feb 1747
> Son to John Thomson, tailor, apprenticed to Alexander Davidson, cooper, 6 years after 8 Dec 1746 - fee £100 Scots.

Thomson, James   31 Dec 1717
> Lawful son to James Thomson at Auchlossen, messenger, apprenticed to James Milne, barber, 3 years from 12 Mar 1710 - fee £36 Scots.

Thomson, James   2 Mar 1730
> Son to Alexander Thomson, farmer in Aberdeen, apprenticed to John Stratton, tailor, 5 years and 1 year from Whitsunday 1726 - fee £30 Scots and a bedding of clothes.

Thomson, Stephen   3 Jun 1744
> Son to the late Stephen Thomson, soldier, a poor boy, apprenticed to James Chalmers, tailor, with consent of the Collector of the Kirk Session, 6 years and 1 year after 8 Nov 1737 - fee £8 Scots.

Touch, Alexander   9 Oct 1733
> Servant to David Wilson of Finzeach, apprenticed to Robert Lamb, weaver, 6 years from Whitsunday 1728 - no fee.

Touch, Alexander   7 Feb 1749
> Son to Alexander Touch, farmer in Lochel, apprenticed to John Still, weaver, 7 years after 10 Jan 1750 - no fee.

Tower, John   1 Jul 1740
> Brother german to James Tower in Miln of Ferryhill, apprenticed to William Moir, cooper, 6 years from 1 Jul 1737 - fee £50 Scots; cautioners, John Tower, merchant and the said James.

Troup, William   1 Apr 1743
> Son to George Troup, farmer at Bowbridge of Aberdeen, apprenticed to Alexander Thomson, shoemaker, 6 years after Martinmas 1742 - fee £3 Stg; cautioners Robert Troup, maltman and Alexander Troup, salmon fisher at Bridge of Dee.

Turner, Andrew   1 Jan 1726
> Son to Robert Turner of Turnerhall, apprenticed to John Carnegie, dyer, 5 years from Mar 1721 - fee 475 merks.

W

Walker, George   6 Mar 1724
> Son to the late James Walker, farmer in Aberdeen, with consent of Thomas Blair, weaver, apprenticed to Alexander Walker, weaver, 5 years from 1 Jan 1720.

Walker, Peter   10 Aug 1710
    Lawful son to the late James Walker, apprenticed to William
    Duckieson, late deacon of the shoemaker trade, 7 years and 1 year
    from 1 Dec 1709.

Wildgoose, James   15 Sep 1750
    Son to the late John Wildgoose in Old Deer, apprenticed to Colin
    Allan, goldsmith, 7 years after 21 Aug 1749 - no fee; Peter
    Turnbull, merchant in Aberdeen, cautioner.

Wilson, George   4 May 1737
    Son to the late George Wilson in Auchleven, apprenticed to Thomas
    Paul, merchant, and present Deal of Guild, 5 years from Martinmas
    last - no fee; cautioners John Tower, merchant, and John Wilson in
    Kirktoun of Clett.   The apprentice to maintain himself in clothing,
    and the master to find him in board, bed and washing, and pay £5 Stg
    for his last year's service.

Windhouse, John   5 Jun 1741
    Son to John Windhouse in Kingshill, apprenticed to Robert Chalmers,
    cooper, 8 years from Martinmas 1733 - no fee.

Wright, George   29 Sep 1726
    Son to George Wright, farmer in Foveran, with advice and consent of
    Alexander Cooper, master of the Music School of Aberdeen,
    apprenticed to James Ferguson, cooper, 6 years and 1 year from 15
    Feb 1722.   Alexander Cooper, cautioner.

Y

Young, Alexander   9 Apr 1726
    Son to the late James Young, weaver in Newtoun of Drennie,
    apprenticed to Alexander Young, weaver, 5 years from 7 Oct 1721.
    William Hadden, weaver in Aberdeen, cautioner for his fidelity.

ROLL OF APPRENTICES
BURGH OF ABERDEEN
1751-1796

INTRODUCTION

Economic and social power in medieval and early modern Scottish burghs lay in the hands of a self-perpetuating oligarchy called burgesses. The rights to operate a business and to vote were limited to these burgesses, who, in order to maintain their priviledges, operated what today would be described as a "closed shop". To become a burgess of Aberdeen, one had to be the son of an existing Aberdeen burgess, marry the daughter of a burgess, buy the right, or serve an apprenticeship under a craftsman or merchant in the burgh. For an apprentice who did not qualify on other grounds, it was of paramount importance that his apprenticeship indenture be recorded to ensure that he became entitled in due course to apply to become a burgess.

Although most Royal Burghs maintained a Register of Indentures, very few have been transcribed and subsequently published. This booklet, laid out in alphabetical order, is based on the work of the Victorian antiquarian Alexander M Munro. It is the third in a series of three.

Frances J McDonnell
St Andrews
January 1994

A

Abel, James   5 Nov 1777
> Son to James Abel in the parish of Kintore, app to William Still, cooper, 5 years after 1 Dec 1772, fee £9 stg.

Abel, William   22 Jul 1784
> Son to Robert Abel, parish of Dyce, app to Margaret Morice & Co, bakers, 5 yrs after Whitsunday 1782, fee £8 stg.   David Morice jr, advocate, cautioner.

Aberdein, Robert   24 Dec 1794
> Son to Thomas Aberdein, in Hillside, parish of Echt, app to James Thomson jr, merchant, 3 years after 1 Jan 1792. Fee £20. The father cautioner.

Adam, Alexander   27 Jun 1789
> Son to Alexander Adam, workman in Aberdeen, app to William Gray, shoemaker, 5 1/2 years from 1 Jun 1784. The father to provide bed, board and lodging for first 2 years.

Adam, James   22 Oct 1793
> Son to John Adam at Upper Mill of Keig, app to John Ross, baker, 5 years from 1 Jan 1790. Fee £5. The father cautioner.

Allan, Alexander   2 May 1785
> Son to James Allan, woolcomber in Aberdeen, app to James Andrew, tailor, 4 years from 4 May 1779. No fee, but a pair of good and sufficient blankets with 15s stg. The father and Alexander Allan, merchant in Turriff, cautioners.

Allan, John   19 Apr 1790
> Son to John Allan, burgess of guild, one of the boys in Gordon's Hospital, app to Nathaniel Gillet, goldsmith, 5 years from 19 May 1785. Fee £100 Scots.

Allan, William   19 Feb 1791
> Son to Alexander Allan at brickkilns in the Links, app to Alexander Ross, yst, merchant, 4 years from 27 Feb 1787. No fee. The father to maintain for first 3 years.

Allardyce, Archibald   31 Oct 1786
> Son to Samuel Allardyce in Lochell, apprenticed to Archibald Reid, baker, 5 years after Whitsunday 1786. Fee £5 stg. His master to maintain him in bed and board.

Allardyce, Joseph   10 Dec 1795
> Son of Samuel Allardyce in Tullochvenus, app to Alexander Thomson,
> cooper, 5 years after 2 Jun 1792. Fee £12. The father cautioner.

Allardyce, William   2 Apr 1796
> Son of Samuel Allardyce in Tullich Venus, parish of Tough,
> apprenticed to William Still jr, cooper, 5 years after 1 Feb 1794.
> Fee £12. The father cautioner.

Anderson, George   2 Feb 1756
> Son to Patrick Anderson at Bucksburn, apprenticed to William
> Johnston, tailor, 5 years after 15 Jun 1751, no fee.

Anderson, George   18 May 1784
> Son of the late Peter Anderson, tailor in Gilcomstone, app to Peter
> Anderson, tailor, 6 years after 1 Jun 1778. No fee. Alex Wallace,
> butcher in Aberdeen, and Peter Sutherland in Auchlee, cautioners.

Anderson, James   1 Aug 1783
> Son to John Anderson, farmer in the parish of Rain, app to Arch Reid,
> baker, 5 years after 17 May 1782. Fee £5 stg. The father and John
> Booth, blacksmith in Aberdeen, cauts. The apprentice to be relieved
> at the end of fourth year on payment of £5 stg to his master.

Anderson, Peter   4 Mar 1778
> Son to John Anderson, resident in Aberdeen, apprenticed to John
> Hadden, tailor, 7 years from 8 Mar 1771. The father and Benjamin
> Anderson, merchant in Aberdeen, cautioners.

Anderson, William   11 May 1781
> Son to Duncan Anderson, gardener at Forresterhill, apprenticed to
> Morice and Co, bakers, 5 years after 1 Apr 1780, fee £8 stg.

Angus, George   12 Nov 1787
> Son of the late James Angus at Skenes Square, app to Peter Gill,
> watchmaker, 6 years from 1 Jan 1782. No fee. Alexander Rough,
> farmer in Cloghill and William Rough, overseer at Udny, cautioners.

Anson, James   30 Nov 1793
> Son of the late David Anson, late horsehirer, one of the boys in the
> Poor's Hospital, apprenticed to Peter Elmslie, shoemaker, 6 years
> from 12 Dec 1787. Fee 10s yearly during apprenticeship. William
> Duncan, schoolmaster, and Samuel Pillar, cowfeeder, cautioners.

B

Bain, James   29 Aug 1793
> Son to the late Farquhar Bain, flaxdresser, apprenticed to William
> Bean, weaver, 7 years after 2 Feb 1789. No fee. John Smith,
> gardener to the Infirmary, cautioner.

Bain, John   8 Dec 1773
    Son to John Bain, sometime in Lochell, appr to John Jaffray, weaver,
    5 years after 1 Dec 1768.   Dr Alexander Robertson, cautioner.
Bain, William   28 Jan 1767
    Son to Andrew Bain in Braeside of Fowlis, apprenticed to John
    Jaffrey, weaver in Aberdeen, 5 years after Candlemas 1762, no fee.
Bannerman, John   22 Feb 1790
    Son to John Bannerman, mason in Aberdeen, apprenticed to Robert
    Smith, merchant, 3 years from 12 Jun 1878, fee £12.
Barclay, George   30 May 1792
    Son to John Barclay, farmer in Echt, apprenticed to William Barclay,
    shoemaker, 6 years from 1 Jun 1787.   The father cautioner.
Barclay, William   11 May 1786
    Son to John Barclay, farmer in Echt, apprenticed to George Paton,
    shoemaker, 5 years after 1 Jun 1781.   No fee.
Barron, John   2 Feb 1786
    Son of the late George Barron, wright, app to George Morison, clock
    and watchmaker, 6 years from 1 Nov 1780.   No fee, but the
    apprentice to uphold himself in bed and board for first two years,
    and in wearing apparel all the time.   Robert Taylor, wright, caut.
Barron, John   13 Aug 1796
    Son of William Barron, farmer in the parish of Insch, apprenticed to
    Alexander Barron,m baker, 5 years after 15 Aug 1791. No fee.
    George McCrundell, merchant, cautioner.
Bartlet, William   16 Apr 1790
    Son of the late James Bartlet, farmer at Frosterhill, app to William
    Knowles, wright, 5 years from 11 Aug 1786.   Fee £10.   George
    Bartlet, farmer in Frosterhill, and James Baillie, merchant, caut.
Bean, James   10 Apr 1782
    Son to the late Alexander Bean, farmer in Mains of Drumbreck,
    apprenticed to William Strachan, baker, 5 years after 4 Jun 1779.
    Fee £7 stg.   George Bean, vintner in Montrose, cautioner.
Beaverly, Alexander   19 Aug 1785
    Son of Alexander Beaverly, tailor, 6 years from 11 Oct 1779.   No
    fee, but £1 stg for bedding of clothes, and the master to provide bed
    and board.   Mr John Leslie, Prof of Greek in King's College, cautioner.
Bennet, John   11 May 1786
    Son to John Bennet, labourer in Aberdeen, apprenticed to James
    Hacket, shoemaker, 5 years after 12 Jun 1781.   No fee.   The father
    and Alexander Stuart, mason, cautioners.
Beverly, Alexander   18 May 1780
    Son to Jas Beverly at Murtle, app to Alex Kemlo, shoemaker, 5 years
    after 6 May 1775. Fee £3 stg, father and Andrew Moir, wright, cauts.

Beverly, James   25 Jan 1791

Son to Andrew Beverly, apprenticed to James Simpson, tailor, 7 years from 1 Jun 1784. No fee. James Beverly, labourer and servant to Gordon's Mills Company, cautioner.

Birse, James   16 Feb 1791

Son to William Birse, in Heughhead of Kincardine O'Neil, appr to Alex Jopp, cooper, 5 years from 15 Dec 1786. Fee £9. Wm Birse in Heughhead, brother, and Magnus Martin, butcher in Aberdeen, cauts.

Black, George   16 Oct 1789

Brother to James Black jn, blacksmith in Footdee, appr to his brother, 5 years from 11 Nov 1784. No fee. James Black, gardener in Banchory, their father, Thomas Black, gardener in Gilcomston, brother to above James, and William Argo, blacksmith, cautioners.

Blaikie, Peter   13 Aug 1790

Son to the late David Blaikie, farmer in Little Dunkeld, apprenticed to John Blaikie, plumber, his brother, 7 years from 1 Aug 1785. No fee. Charles Cooper, blacksmith in Aberdeen, cautioner.

Booth, James   5 Jul 1792

Son of John Booth, blacksmith in Aberdeen, apprenticed to Alexander Booth, merchant, 5 years from 7 Sep 1787. The master to pay £5 for the last year of apprenticeship.

Brown, John   2 Jan 1778

Son to William Brown, woolcomber in Aberdeen, apprenticed to Walter Paul, shoemaker, 5 years after 4 Jan 1773. The father and James Brown, woolcomber, cautioners.

Brown, Robert   7 Aug 1793

Son of George Brown in Logie, app to Charles Farquharson, merchant, 7 years after Martinmas 1787. Fee £10. The father cautioner.

Browster, Alexander   19 Feb 1789

Son to the late Alexander Browster in Colonach, app to Dorothy Smith, alias Martin, relict of the late Robert Martin, baker, 5 years from 17 Feb 1789. Fee £5. William Donald in Colonach, cautioner.

Buck, Andrew   21 May 1795

Son to the late Joseph Buck, cartwright at Tollahill, app to Alexander Anderson, shoemaker, 5 years after 1 Jun 1790. No fee. John Murray in Jockston, cautioner.

Burgess, Alexander   22 Jul 1784

Son to Alexander Burgess in New Mill of Keith, app to Margaret Morice and Company, bakers, 5 years from 1 Feb 1781. Fee £10 stg.

Burnett, Nathaniel   22 mar 1783

Son to Alexander Burnett, gardener in Hardgate, app to John Wallace, baker, 5 years after 15 April, 1778. Fee £5 stg with wearing apparel. The father and Alexander Scott, wright, cautioners.

Burnett, Thomas   15 Jul 1788
    Son to Alexander Burnett, gardener in the Hardgate, app to William
    Seaton, baker, 5 years from 1 Nov 1785. Fee £6. The father and
    Alexander Burnett, clerk to Alexander Scott, wright, cautioners.

C

Cadenhead, William   29 Aug 1787
    Son to Robert Cadenhead in Robertson, app to Peter Robertson,
    staymaker in Aberdeen, 5 years after 23 Aug 1782. Fee £8 6s 8d.
    Apprentice to uphold himself in clothes, washing and other
    necessaries, the master to maintain in bed and board. Robert
    Cadenhead, servant to Lewis Wilson, tailor, and Magnus Martin,
    butcher, cautioners.
Caie, Robert   5 Feb 1791
    Son to Robert Caie, brickmaker, Old Aberdeen, app to John Nicoll &
    Co ironmongers, 4 yrs from 26 Mar 1787, fee £13 and a bedding of
    clothes. Father and George Davidson, wright, Gordon's Mills, cauts.
Calder, John   13 Jan 1796
    Son of the late William Calder, tailor, one of the boys educated in
    the Poors Hospital, apprenticed to Donald McDonald, tailor, 6 years
    after 23 Feb 1790, fee 10s yearly. Master of the Hospital, caut.
Campbell, Alexander   1 May 1751
    Son to Malcolm Campbell, tailor in Aberdeen, apprenticed to John
    Duthie, wright, 8 years after 5 May 1750, no fee; George Main,
    shoemaker and Alexander Tough, clothseller, cautioners.
Carnegie, John   26 Sep 1754
    Son to the late James Carnegie, dyer, with consent of Mary Thomson,
    his mother, app to Dr James and Dr John Gregorys, Physicians in
    Aberdeen, 2 or 3 years in option of employers, after Martinmas
    1751, fee £200 Scots; James Thomson of Portlethen, cautioner.
Carse, Cochran   28 Aug 1782
    Son to Wm Carse, preacher of the gospel at Red Kirk of Portlethen,
    app to Robert Martin, baker, 5 years after 26 May 1779, fee £5 stg.
Cassie, William   4 Sep 1760
    Son to John Cassie, wright, apprenticed to William Robertson,
    weaver, 7 years after 12 Jun 1756, no fee.
Cassie, William   6 Sep 1789
    Resident in Aberdeen, apprenticed to Alexander Walker, skinner, 5
    years from 4 Dec 1784. No fee. William Craik, resident, and
    William Cassie, resident and father to the apprentice, cautioners.

Catto, Robert   27 Feb 1793
    Son of the late Charles Catto, sometime wright in Foveran,
    apprenticed to Catto and Reid, merchants, 4 years from 1 Apr 1790.
    No fee.   Robert Black, farmer in Auchnacant, cautioner.
Catto, William   28 Feb 1755
    Son to William Catto, weaver, apprenticed to George Simson, tailor,
    7 years after 15 Jun 1751, no fee.
Chalmers, Andrew   1 Feb 1758
    Son to Walter Chalmers in Udny, app to David Turreff, wright, 5
    years after Martinmas 1755, fee £5 5s with a bedding of clothes.
Chalmers, James   3 Jun 1768
    Son to late Mr Patrick Chalmers in Strathbogy, app to Jas Kemp, shoe
    maker, 3 yrs after 1 May 1765, no fee, Hugh Chalmers, brother caut.
Chalmers, Robert   6 Apr 1762
    Son to Robert Chalmers at Miln of Sclattie, app to George Simson,
    tailor, 6 years after Martinmas 1757.   Fee £2 stg.   Alexander
    Chalmers in Slattie and the said Robert Chalmers cautioners.
Chalmers, William   8 Nov 1794
    Son to the late John Chalmers, late farmer in Ardmore, apprenticed
    to George Hogg, merchant, 4 years after 7 Dec 1790.   Fee £12.
    Alexander Roberson, merchant, cautioner.
Chapman, William   2 May 1785
    Son of George Chapman, weaver in Aberdeen, one of the boys
    educated in Robert Gordon's Hospital, app to William Stivinson,
    weaver, 5 years from 1 Jan 1781.   Fee, £100 Scots payable by
    Hospital, the father to uphold his son in clothes, washing and other
    necessaries, the master to maintain the apprentice in board.
Chillas, Robert   9 Sep 1760
    Son to late Alex Chillas, sometime in Littledovie, with consent of
    Robert Chillas, in Mains of Littledovie, his uncle, app to Alex Smith,
    merchant, 6 years after Whitsunday 1752, no fee.
Chisholm, James   8 Feb 1773
    Son to Alexander Chisholm, late soldier in the King's service, now
    resident in Aberdeen, apprenticed to Alexander Cruickshank,
    shoemaker, 5 1/2 years after 12 Aug 1767.   Fee £2 stg.   The father
    and Charles Farquharson in Gilcomston cautioners.
Christie, James   5 Nov 1777
    Son to James Christie, farmer at Gallowgate Head, apprenticed to
    Patrick Gordon, saddler, 7 years after 1 Dec 1770.
Christie, John   15 Sep 1761
    Son to Alexander Christie, miller at Kildrimmie, app to John Forbes,
    baker, 5 yrs after Whitsun 1759.   Fee £5 stg and bedding of clothes,
    and if he incline to serve other two years he is to get back the fee.

Christie, William   16 Dec 1788
   Son to James Christie, farmer in Aberdeen, apprenticed to James
   Christie, saddler, 5 years from 10 Oct 1784.   Fee £5.
Clark, George   25 Jul 1791
   Son to William Clark in Tofthills, parish of Kintore, apprenticed to
   James Downie, shoemaker, 5 years from 21 Dec 1786. Fee £5.   The
   father and John Duncan at Rubislaw, cautioners.
Clark, William   7 Jul 1792
   Son of the late George Clark, tailor, apprenticed to William and
   James Christie, saddlers, 6 1/2 years from 7 Jul 1790.   Fee £100
   Scots.   Alexander Ainslie, shoemaker, Denburn, cautioner.
Clerihue, Alexander   24 May 1755
   Son to John Clerihue at Wood of Putachie, with consent of James
   Lord Forbes, apprenticed to John Sligo jr, wheelwright, 5 years after
   1 Jun 1752, fee £3 stg, with a sufficient bedding of clothes.   Lord
   Forbes and John Clerihue, cautioners.
Clerk, James   24 Sep 1787
   Son of Gilbert Clerk, late mason in Aberdeen, now in Jamaica, with
   consent of Isobel Gauld, his mother, apprenticed to Charles Lunan,
   clock and watch maker, 9 years after 1 Jan 1779.   No fee.   Thomas
   Gordon, mason, and James Thain, wright, cautioners.
Clerk, John   9 Oct 1780
   Son to the late Alexander Clerk, late mariner in Aberdeen,
   app to James Murray, baker, 5 years after Whitsunday 1776. William
   Leith in Froghall and Alexander Gordon in Kinavird, New Deer, cauts.
Clerk, John   5 Dec 1792
   Son of Peter Clerk in Tillerneer, apprenticed to Andrew Wilson,
   wright, 5 years from 14 Dec 1787.   Fee £6.   Cautioner, the father.
Collie, James   23 May 1796
   Son to Jas Collie, woolcomber, app to Geo Stott, weaver, 5 years
   after 4 Jun 1791.   No fee, the father and John Begbie, carver, cauts.
Collie, William   11 Nov 1778
   Son to Robert Collie in Nether Park of Culter, apprenticed to Patrick
   Durward, baker, 5 years after 10 Jun 1774.   Fee £112. 12s Scots.
   John Collie in Bogtown of Drum cautioner.
Conon, Andrew   23 Aug 1766
   Son to the late John Connon at Miln of Tipperty, apprenticed to David
   Walker, cooper, 6 years after 6 Dec 1765.   No fee, but a bedding of
   clothes.   Thomas Cassie, at the Miln of Foveran, cautioner.
Cooper, Charles   5 Nov 1777
   Son to John Cooper, mason in Inverury, appenticed to James Thain,
   blacksmith, 5 years after Martinmas 1772.

7

Aberdeen Apprentices

Cooper, John   24 Feb 1781
Son to the late John Cooper, shoemaker in Aberdeen, apprenticed to
James Hunter, merchant, 6 years after 1 Mar 1775, no cautioner.

Cordiner, John   11 May 1786
Son to William Cordiner, in March Marr, in the parish of Kearn,
apprenticed to John Wallace, baker, 5 years after 1 Jun 1781.   Fee
£4 stg.   The father and Alexander Walker in Drumnahive, cautioners.

Courage, Arthur   29 Jul 1752
Son to Arthur Courage in Keir of Belhelvie, app to Wm Moir, cooper, 6
years after 17 Jul 1747, fee 100 merks;   George Courage, Keir, caut.

Courage, James   24 Sep 1791
Son of James Courage at Silverburn, app to John Lamb, wright, 5
years from 12 May 1790.   Fee £8 stg and £1 to buy tools.   James
Courage sr. cautioner.

Coutts, John   1 Jan 1796
Son to Jas Coutts, weaver, app to Wm Leitch, coppersmith, 5 years
after 4 Jan1791, fee £10.   Father and Joseph Berry, weaver, cauts.

Coutts, William   27 Mar 1793
Son to James Coutts, flaxdresser, app to Peter Priest, cutler, 5 yrs
from 22 Nov1788, fee £5.   Father and John Johnston merchant,cauts.

Cowie, William   1 Mar 1785
Son of the late Wm Cowie, wright, app to Wm Farquharson, saddler, 5
years from 4 Jun 1780.   Consent of John Copland, present Treasurer
of Robert Gordon's Hospital, who undertakes to pay the fee of £8 6s
8d stg in respect of Marr being a boy educated in the Hospital.   Jos
Forbes, wright, and Robert Morison, Town Drummer, cautioners.

Crives, William   30 Jul 1792
Son to the late William Crives at Silverburn, apprenticed to William
Michie, wright, 5 years from 1 Jan 1791.   Fee £7 with a bed and
bedding of clothes.   Alexander Gill at Foulpool, Thomas Gordon,
mason, and Andrew Lawson, blacksmith in Old Aberdeen, cautioners.

Cromar, Alexander   31 Oct 1795
Son of the late William Cromar in Abereen, apprenticed to George
Henderson, weaver, 5 years after 1 Jun 1791.   No fee.   Andrew
Tawse, flaxdresser in Aberdeen, cautioner.

Cromar, James   28 Feb 1755
Son to John Cromar in Braeside of Forbes, apprenticed to James
Nivie, merchant, 5 years after Whitsunday 1750, no fee;   John
Taylor, advocate in Aberdeen cautioner.

Crombie, Alexander   5 Nov 1777
Son to Alexander Crombie in Berryhillock, apprenticed to George
Davidson, cooper, 5 years after 16 Nov 1772.   Fee £10 1s stg.   The
father and James Nicoll, merchant, cautioners.

Cruickshank, George   3 Mar 1786
    Son to George Cruickshank, labourer in Aberdeen, apprenticed to John
    Wallace, shoemaker, 5 years from 1 Jun 1781.   Fee £1 stg.   The
    father and John Murray, farmer in Jackston, cautioners.
Cruickshank, John   23 May 1787
    Son of John Cruickshank, farmer at Millbuie, parish of Skene,
    app to Adam Watt, baker, 5 years after 1 Mar 1786.   Fee £5 stg.
Cruickshank, William   29 Jul 1752
    Son to James Cruickshank, shoemaker, apprenticed to Andrew Aiken,
    barber, 7 years after 6 Jun 1746, no fee.
Cruickshank, William   30 Jan 1778
    Son to James Cruickshank, shoemaker in Aberdeen, apprenticed to
    James Farquhar, shoemaker, 5 years after 14 Feb 1773.   The father
    and Alexander Cruickshank, shoemaker, cautioners.
Cruickshank, William   21 May 1791
    Son to George Cruickshank, resident, apprenticed to John Wallace,
    shoemaker, 5 years from 5 Jun 1786.   Fee £1.   The father and John
    Murray, farmer in Ardo, cautioners.
Cushnie, William   1 Dec 1794
    Son to John Cushnie, Glashmore, app to William Seton, baker, 5
    years.   Fee £3.   The father and Peter Cushnie, Mains of Drum, cauts.
Cushny, Thomas   27 May 1765
    Son to Patrick Cushny, merchant in Stonehaven, apprenticed to
    George Copland, cooper, 5 years after 1 Jun 1760, fee £5 stg.

D

Dalgarno, Alexander   12 Mar 1790
    Son of the late Alexander Dalgarno, manufacturer in Peterhead,
    apprenticed to Charles Walker, merchant, 5 years from 25 Jun 1785.
    No fee.   James Dalgarno, merchant in Peterhead, cautioner.
Dauney, James   4 Apr 1778
    Son to James Dauney in Glasgow Forrest, apprenticed to Thomas
    Abel, baker, 5 years after Martinmas 1774.
Dauney, William   27 Apr 1793
    Son to William Dauney, in Finnylost, parish of Strathdon, app to
    James Dauney, shoemaker, 5 years from 19 Jun 1788.   Fee £5.
    The father and Wm McCook in Colquharrie, parish of Strathdon, cauts.
Davidson, Alexander   24 Nov 1785
    Son of John Davidson, at Newbigging near Drumlithie, apprenticed to
    Adam Watt, baker, 5 years from 1 May 1780.   Fee £5 stg.   The
    father and Alexander Mason, vintner, cautioners.

Davidson, Alexander   29 Aug 1787
Son of the late Alex Davidson in Shiells, app to Peter Robertson,
staymaker, 8 years after 30 Jun 1780. No fee. Master to maintain
in bed and board. George Davidson, servant to George Murdoch in
Lawrencekirk, and John Bothwell, woolcomber in Aberdeen, cauts.

Davidson, Andrew   15 Sep 1761
Son to the late John Davidson in Couperston, apprenticed to Thomas
Taylor, wright, for 5 years after Martinmas 1756. Apprentice fee
£7 stg with a bedding of clothes. James Kilgour, gardener in Old
Aberdeen, and Christan Davidson, relict of said John, cautioners.

Davidson, Robert   9 May 1771
Son to Alexander Davidson in Mains of Clakriack, apprenticed to
William Allan, clock and watchmaker, 5 years after 14 Aug 1766.
Fee £8 stg and a bedding of clothes. Thomas Bruce, stabler in
Aberdeen, and James Davidson in Clakriack, cautioners.

Davidson, William   30 Sep 1761
Son to William Davidson in Bogheads of Kintore, app to John Morrice,
baker, 5 years after Martinmas, 1757. No fee, the father cautioner.

Davidson, William   7 Mar 1793
Son of Thomas Davidson, weaver, a boy in Robert Gordon's Hospital,
app to John Leslie, goldsmith jeweller, 5 yrs after 20 Apr 1789, fee
£100 Scots. Father and John Copland, treasurer of the Hospital, cauts.

Deack, Alexander   11 May 1781
Son to William Deack in Weetloans, apprenticed to Adam Wall, baker,
5 years after 26 May 1777. Fee £7 stg. John Deack, mason and
Frederick Thomson, resident in Aberdeen, cautioners.

Diack, James   18 Feb 1782
Son to the late Alexander Diack, farmer in Mickle Wartle,
apprenticed to Alexander Jopp, cooper, 5 years after 21 Nov 1777.
Fee £10 stg. Alexander Diack, farmer in Mickle Wartle, cautioner.

Donald, Andrew   7 Jul 1792
Son of James Donald in Mill of Dalpersie, apprenticed to James
Christie, saddler, 6 years from 9 Apr 1789. Fee £5 10s. The father
and Arthur Milner, merchant, cautioners.

Donald, James   28 Mar 1793
Son of James Donald, woolcomber, app to Alexander Titler,
shoemaker, 5 years from 14 Apr 1788. No fee. The father caut.

Douglas, James   4 Mar 1778
Son to John Douglas in Fauch Inch, apprenticed to James Nowall,
shoemaker, 5 years after 5 Mar 1773, fee £1 10s stg.

Dun, David   10 Aug 1790
Son to Robert Dun, teacher of dancing, apprenticed to John Imray,
baker, 5 years from 16 Aug 1785. Fee £6 10s.

Dunbar, John   4 Nov 94
Son of James Dunbar, shoemaker, app to George Stott, weaver, 5 yrs after Martinmas 1789, no fee.   Father and Wm Griach, mason, cauts.
Duncan, Alexander   10 Apr 1782
Son to John Duncan in the parish of Daviot, app to Wm Strachan, baker, 5 yrs after 5 Jan1780, fee £9 stg.   James Duncan,Daviot, caut.
Duncan, James   20 Feb 1778
Son to James Duncan, mason in Aberdeen, app to George Strachan, shoemaker, 5 years from 24 February 1783.   No fee.   The father to maintain for first 15 months, and pay £1 for a bedding of clothes.
Duncan, James   19 Feb 1789
Son to Alex Duncan, app to John Wallace, baker, 4 yrs from 17 Aug 1785.   Fee £8.
Duncan, James   20 Jan 1796
Son to John Duncan, carter, app to Peter Simpson, merchant, 4 1/2 years after 21 Jul 1791.   No fee.   The father cautioner.   Assigned by consent of the parties to George Daniel, merchant, 5 Nov 1792.
Duncan, John   28 Aug 1782
Son to the late John Duncan in the parish of Daviot, app to William Strachan, baker, 5 years after 1 Feb 1781.   Fee £9 stg.   Alexander Duncan, apprentice to the said William Strachan, caut.
Duncan, John   23 May 1787
Son of Andrew Duncan, residing in Old Aberdeen, apprenticed to Adam Watt, baker, 7 years after Whitsunday, 1780.   No fee, the master to maintain in bed, board and lodging.
Duncan, Livingston   17 Nov 1780
Son of late Alex Duncan in Cults, app to Wm Neilson, butcher, 5 years after Martinmas 1779.   William Gordon, merchant in Aberdeen, caut.
Duncan, Nicholas   11 Nov 1778
Son to Robert Duncan jr, merchant in Aberdeen, apprenticed to John Smith, wright, 5 years after 29 Sep 1777.
Durward, Alexander   17 Jun 1790
Son of the late William Durward, late merchant in Aberdeen, one of the boys in Gordon's Hospital, apprenticed to John Smith, wright, 5 years from 20 Jun 1785.   Fee £100 Scots.   Christian Burnett, his mother, and Charles Copland, merchant, cautioners.
Durward, Charles   10 Jan 1769
Son to John Durward, resident in Aberdeen, apprenticed to William Bennet, saddler, 6 years after 1 Apr 1763, fee £6 stg.
Durward, George   10 Dec 1764
Son to John Durward, resident in Aberdeen, apprenticed to Benjamin Cruikshank, wright, 5 years from 1 Jan 1760.   No fee.   Dr James Forbes, Robert Thomson, town clerk, and the father cautioners.

Duthie, William   18 Nov 1794
    Son of John Duthie, tailor, apprenticed to John Webster, weaver, 5
    years after 1 Dec 1789. Fee £2. The father cautioner.
Dyce, Philip   13 Oct 1770
    Son to the late Thomas Dyce, weaver in this burgh, app to Alexander
    Ross, butcher, 5 years after Candlemas, master to pay £1 15s stg
    yearly and to maintain the apprentice in bed, board and washing.
Dyce, William   2 May 1785
    Son of Peter Dyce, wood sawer in Aberdeen, apprenticed to Thomas
    Taylor, wright, 5 years after 1 Jun 1780. No fee.

E

Elmslie, John   12 Feb 1795
    Son of Alexander Elmslie, servant to Strachan, Imray and Company at
    the Newbridge, apprenticed to William Strachan, baker, 5 years after
    12 Aug 1794. No fee. The father cautioner.
Emslie, John   24 Nov 1781
    Son to William Emslie, late farmer in Tolmelie, in the parish of
    Cushnie, apprenticed to William French, baker, 5 years after 13 Dec
    1779. Fee £7 stg. James Emslie, farmer in Tolmelie cautioner.
England, Seton   24 May 1755
    Son to Alex England in Achentyne, app to Robert Thom, blacksmith, 5
    years after 1 Jun 1752, no fee; James England in Easter Ardo and
    Alexander England, journeyman blacksmith in Aberdeen, cautioners.
Erskine, James   2 Feb 1787
    Son to late James Erskine, late vintner in Aberdeen, with consent of
    his mother, appr to James Smith, goldsmith, 6 yrs after 10 Sep1781.
    No fee, to maintain himself in bed and board for 3 yrs.
Esson, John   6 Apr 1761
    Son to Thomas Esson in Gilcomston, apprenticed to William Forbes,
    coppersmith, 9 years after 24 Nov 1760, no fee.

F

Falconer, Alexander   23 May 1782
    Son to John Falconer in Ashintilly in the parish of Durris,
    apprenticed to William Law, baker, 5 years after 5 Dec 1781.
Farquharson, Donald   5 Nov 1777
    Son to the late John Farquharson in Borrowston, app to Alex
    Henderson, wright, 5 years after 1 Dec 1772, fee £5 stg, the mother
    cautioner.

Farskin, William   18 May 1784
> Son to James Farskin, in Woodend, apprenticed to Alexander Morison, cooper, 5 years after 15 Mar 1781. Fee £10 stg. The father and James Andrew, tailor in Aberdeen, cautioners.

Ferguson, Charles   20 Nov 1786
> Son to William Ferguson, labourer in Aberdeen, apprenticed to George Milne, shoemaker, 5 years after 3 Dec 1781. No fee. The father and John Gilchrist, labourer, cautioners.

Ferguson, John   18 May 1784
> Son to late John Ferguson, cooper in Aberdeen, app to David Walker, cooper, 6 years after 12 Jul 1779. Fee £10 stg and a bedding of clothes. Wm Burnet, advocate and James Mason, baker, cauts.

Fettes, James   7 Aug 1793
> Son of the late Alexander Fettes, cartwright in Old Aberdeen, app to Margaret Morice, baker, 5 years after 8 Jan 1792. Fee £5. Mary Ogston, his mother and William Christie, saddler, cautioners.

Fettes, John   10 May 1793
> Son of William Fettes, salmon fisher at Bridge of Don, apprenticed to John Wallace, baker, 5 years from 22 May 1788. Fee £6. Cautioners, the father and John Hector, resident.

Findlay, John   26 Sep 1760
> Son to Robert Findlay, nailmaker, apprenticed to William Forbes, coppersmith, 8 years after 10 Nov 1748, no fee.

Findlayson, John   23 Jul 1778
> Son to Eric Findlayson, resident in Aberdeen, app to James Simson, tailor, 7 years after 1 Sep 1777. The father and David Lindsay, weaver, cautioners.

Finnie, George   25 Nov 1789
> Son to George Finnie, burgess of guild, one of the boys of Robert Gordon's Hospital, apprenticed to William Dawson, tailor, 5 years from 5 Dec 1784. Fee £100 Scots. The father and Robert McPherson in Old Aberdeen cautioners.

Fleming, George   6 Apr 1792
> Son of Jas Fleming, mason in Aberdeen, app to Garvock & White, stay·makers, 7 yrs from 7 Apr1785.Father and Jas Thomson,writer, cauts.

Fleming, William   14 Aug 1760
> Son to John Freeman, weaver, apprenticed to John Ferguson, cooper, 5 years after 11 Apr 1759, no fee.

Forbes, James   30 Jul 1792
> Son to George Forbes, tailor burgess, apprenticed to James Clerk, tailor, present Factor to Miln's Mortification, belonging to the Tailor trade, 5 years from Martinmas 1787. Fee £2 10s to be paid out of said mortification. Charles Mackie, tailor, cautioner.

Forbes, Thomas   27 Mar 1780
Son to late Rev Mr William Forbes, minister of the Gospel at Airth,
and Elizabeth Garioch, his relict, resident in Aberdeen, app to
Kenneth Mackenzie, merchant, 5 years after 1 Apr1775. Mother caut.

Forbes, William   1 Feb 1752
Son to Mr Alexander Forbes in Hearthills, apprenticed to George
Cooper, goldsmith, 7 years after Martinmas 1745, no fee.

Forbes, William   19 Jan 1782
Son to Hugh Forbes of Shevas, apprenticed to William Ritchie,
merchant, 4 years after 28 Aug 1781, fee £60 stg.

Forsyth, Alexander   22 Aug 1795
Son of John Forsyth, merchant in Elgin, apprenticed to George Sim,
saddler, 5 years after 1 Nov 1790. Fee £16. The father cautioner.

Fraser, Alexander   12 May 1760
Son to John Fraser in Causeway End, apprenticed to William
Johnston, tailor, 5 years after 20 May 1755, no fee.

Fraser, Alexander   17 Jan 1781
Son to Alexander Fraser, labourer in Aberdeen, apprenticed to
William Reid, shoemaker, 5 years after 22 Jan 1776, fee £4 10s.

Fraser, James   8 Feb 1773
Son to Robert Fraser, maltster at Newbridge, app to Geo Williamson,
butcher, 5 years from 19 March 1772. Geo Leslie, merchant, caut.

Fraser, William   1 Jun 1779
Son of the late James Fraser, late in Rottenbogs, apprenticed to
Peter Robertson, staymaker, 6 years after 16 Jun 1773. Fee £5 5s
stg. Lewis Fraser, gardener in London, now in Aberdeen, cautioner.

Freeman, William   2 Feb 1756
Son to William Freeman, boatman, apprenticed to Robert Memis,
cooper, 5 years after 22 Jul 1754, no fee.

French, Edward   11 Dec 1789
Son of the late Edward French, weaver, apprenticed to Alexander
Paterson, shoemaker, 5 years from 1 Jan 1785. Fee £100 Scots, he
being one of the boys of Robert Gordon's Hospital. William Dewar,
merchant, and William Duncan, Master of the Workhouse, cautioners.

Frost, John   20 Apr 1787
Son of the late James Frost, late merchant in Auchindore,
apprenticed to John Meff, weaver, 5 years after 25 Feb 1783. No
fee, his master to uphold him in bed, board, wearing apparel and
washing. Alexander Frost, flaxdresser in Aberdeen, cautioner.

G

Gall, James   22 Jul 1784
   Son to William Gall in Little Wartle, apprenticed to Alexander Jopp,
   cooper, 5 years - contract dated 6 Oct 1780. Fee £9 stg.
Garden, Andrew   21 May 1766
   Son to Robert Garden, apprenticed to Alexander Kemp, weaver, 5
   years after this date, fee £2 stg.
Garvock, Robert   9 Nov 1790
   Son of James Garvock, salmon fisher, and grandson of Alex Davidson,
   burgess of guild, a boy from Gordon's Hospital, apprenticed to Alex
   Ferguson, tailor, 5 years from 15 Dec 1785. Fee £100 Scots.
Gavin, George   1 Dec 1756
   Son to John Gavin, merchant in Newburgh, apprenticed to Alexander
   Rose, cabinetmaker in Ellon, 5 years after 26 Jun 1755, fee £10 stg.
Gellan, Alexander   3 Mar 1786
   Son to Alexander Gellan, butcher in Aberdeen, apprenticed to John
   Wallace, shoemaker, 5 years from 12 Apr, 1781. No fee. The father
   and John Henderson, woolcomber, cautioners
Gibson, Alexander   20 Jan 1788
   Son to James Gibson in Links, parish of Old Machar, apprenticed to
   John Wallace, baker, 4 years from Candlemas 1784. Fee 8. The
   father and George Symers, farmer in Upper Torrie, cautioners.
Gibson, James   30 Sep 1761
   Son to Alexander Gibson in Coothill of Slains, apprenticed to
   Alexander Mortimer, upholsterer, 5 years after 1 Apr last, no fee,
   and the master is to pay the apprentice eighteenpence stg of wages.
Gibson, James   15 Jul 1772
   Son to James Gibson, labourer in Aberdeen, apprenticed to James
   Neilson, butcher, 7 years after Whitsunday 1772. The father and
   Alexander Elmslie, labourer, cautioners.
Gibson, William   10 Jun 1790
   Son to Wm Gibson in Hassacks, a boy from Gordon's Hospital, app to
   Geo Smith, glazier, 5 years from 11 Apr 1786. Fee £100 Scots.
Gillet, Hugh   2 Feb 1786
   Son of the late James Gillet, late schoolmaster in Aberdeen,
   apprenticed to George Morison, clock and watchmaker, 6 years after
   1 Jun 1783. John Copland, treasurer of Robert Gordon's Hospital,
   bound for fee of £100 Scots, and the apprentice to uphold himself in
   wearing apparel. William Farquharson, saddler, cautioner.
Gordon, George   22 Apr 1788
   Son to Geo Gordon in Boginclock, app to Jas Gordon & Co, jewellers, 7
   yrs from Whitsun1781, no fee. Patrick Gordon saddler,Aberdeen,caut.

Gordon, George   20 Jun 1795
> Son to Geo Gordon, blacksmith in the Hardgate, app to Wm Littlejohn, wright, 6 years after 26 Aug 1789. No fee. The father caut.

Gordon, John   23 May 1782
> Son to Thomas Gordon, woolcomber in Aberdeen, apprenticed to William Simpson, tailor, 5 years after 20 Jun 1777. Fee 3 stg. The father and William Smith, slater, cautioners.

Gordon, John   2 Jan 1795
> Son to late John Gordon in Newton of Coharoie, app to Jas Finnie, wright, 5 years after 1 May 1791. fee £12 12s. John Gordon Esq of Craigmile, cautioner.

Gordon, Lewis   12 May 1795
> Son of Alexander Gordon, late in Dykehead of Belnabodach, apprenticed to John Gordon, merchant, 5 years after Whitsunday 1790. No fee. Robert Ogg, square wright, cautioner.

Gordon, Peter   2 Jan 1778
> One of the boys in the Poors Hospital, apprenticed to Alexander Cruickshank, shoemaker, 5 years from 10 Jan 1777. Fee 10s yearly. Mr Andrew Johnston, principal master of the said Hospital cautioner.

Gordon, Robert   23 Jul 1778
> Son of Jas Gordon in Meldrum, app to Jas Gordon,jeweller/goldsmith, 6 years after 1 Aug 1772. Patrick Gordon, saddler, Aberdeen caut.

Gordon, Robert   1 Mar 1796
> Son of John Gordon, sometime mariner, apprenticed to John Lamb, wright, with consent of Janet Martin, his mother, Andrew Hall, bucher, and John Kynoch, farmer, 5 years after 26 Oct 1791. No fee. The above persons cautioners.

Gordon, Thomas   11 Apr 1760
> Son to James Gordon in Forgue, apprenticed to George Simson, cooper in Aberdeen, 6 years after 21 Jun 1754 fee £10 stg; Alexander Banerman, merchant in Aberdeen cautioner.

Gordon, Thomas   30 Jul 1792
> Son of James Gordon, labourer in Gilcomston, apprenticed to James Robson, merchant, 5 years from 1 Aug 1787. The father, Thomas Gordon, labourer in Aberdeen, Alexander Gordon, turner in Gilcomston, and Alexander Robertson, labourer, cautioners.

Gordon, William   28 Sep 1795
> Son of Alexander Gordon in Knock of Glenmuick, app to Wm Leys, cooper, 4 years after 6 Jul 1792. Fee £16. The father cautioner.

Grant, Duncan   11 Dec 1782
> Son to John Grant, tailor in Aberdeen, apprenticed to Alexander Fiddes, weaver, 5 years after Whitsunday 1781.

Grant, John   11 May 1786
    Son to Alexander Grant, saddler in Aberdeen, apprenticed to George
    Strachan, shoemaker, 5 1/2 years after 1 Dec 1780. No fee. The
    father and James Forbes, shoemaker, cautioners.
Gray, James   4 Apr 1778
    Son to George Gray in Nigg, app to Alex Davidson, butcher, 6 years
    after Whitsun 1772.   Alex Gray, workman in Aberdeen, cautioner.
Gray, John   8 Nov 1793
    Son to late James Gray in Traylodge, app to John Wallace, baker, 4
    years from 1 Dec 1789. Fee £8.   John Hunter in Confunderland caut.
Greenlaw, William   20 Sep 1793
    Son of the late William Greenlaw in Castlehill, apprenticed to James
    Gordon and Company, goldsmiths, 7 years after 4 Dec 1787. No fee.
    William Hector in Muir of Rynie, cautioners.

H

Hacket, James   29 Nov 1762
    Son to George Hacket, labourer, app to Francis Gordon, shoemaker, 5
    years after 30 Nov 1761. No fee, but a bedding of clothes.   The
    father and William Hacket, farmer in Aberdeen, cautioners.
Hall, Alexander   28 Aug 1782
    Son to the late Geo Hall in Mains of Grange, app to Robert Martin,
    baker, 5 years after Jun 1780.   Fee £5, John Thain, Drumblair, caut.
Harrow, Thomas   28 Feb 1755
    Son to Jas Harrow, salmon fisher at the Brickkilns of Aberdeen, app
    to Geo Wright, cooper, 5 years after Candlemas 1755, fee £8 stg,
    with a bedding of clothes; John his brother and William Craig in
    Ruthrieston, cautioners.
Harrow, William   1 Jun 1779
    Son to George Harrow, salmon fisher in Aberdeen, apprenticed to
    James Gerard, cooper, 5 years after 20 Jun 1774.   Fee £100 Scots,
    payable by the Treasurer of Robert Gordon's Hospital.
Harvie, William   18 Apr 1785
    Son to the late James Harvie, farmer in Fintray, with consent of
    John Harvie, clerk to John Watson, Common Brewer, and Alexander
    Chalmers, wright, app to William Knowles, wright, 5 years, contract
    dated 10 Jun 1780.   Fee £2 10s stg and a bedding of clothes.
Henderson, James   29 Apr 1793
    Son to William Henderson in Auchlunies, app to Wm Bain, weaver, 5
    years after 28 May 1791.   Fee 2 bolls of meal.   The father caut.

Henderson, John   2 Feb 1786
    Son of Andrew Henderson, parish of Ellon, app to Wm Knowls,weaver,
    5 yrs from 10 Nov 1784, no fee. John Chrystall, merchant, caut.
Henderson, William   1 Feb 1758
    Son to Patrick Henderson, cooper in Lutingston, parish of Rathen, app
    to Andrew Mathison, weaver, 5 years after Whitsun 1753, no fee.
Henderson, William   2 May 1785
    Residing in Aberdeen, apprenticed to Alexander Morison, cooper, 5
    years from 3 Aug 1783.   The apprentice for the first 2 years to
    maintain himself in bed and board, and the master to maintain him
    for the remaining period.   Alexander Henderson, merchant, cautioner.
Hogg, Francis   9 Sep 1760
    Son to John Hogg, farmer in Lumphan, apprenticed to John Hadden,
    tailor, 7 years after 2 Sep 1755, £8 Scots paid as fee by the
    Collector of the Church Session.
Hogg, Robert   22 Jul 1784
    In Barns of Durris, with consent of Alex Hogg there, his brother, app
    to Robert Martin, baker, 5 years from 7 Apr 1782, fee £5 stg.
Hope, James   6 Mar 1775
    Son to John Hope, Chelsea pensioner in Aberdeen, apprenticed to
    James Nowall, shoemaker, 5 years after 20 Mar 1770.   The father
    and John Still, merchant, cautioners.
Horn, Robert   12 May 1793
    Son to the late John Horn in Old Meldrum, apprenticed to Robert
    Birnie, tanner and currier, 5 years after 13 Aug 1789.   No fee.
    Joseph Berry, weaver and Alexander Shand, miller, cautioners.
Horn, William   28 Nov 1795
    Son of Jas Horn in Mill of Bonnytown, parish of Rayne, app to Wm
    Logan, merchant, 3 years after 1 Dec 1792. Fee £10, the father caut.
Howie, Alexander   23 May 1787
    Son of Geo Howie, late dyer in Hardgate, app to James Hacket,
    shoemaker, 5 years after 18 Jun 1782.   Fee £5 5s stg and bedding of
    clothes.   The father and Robert Balmanno, feuar at Robslaw, cauts.

I

Imlay, Hugh   22 Jun 1782
    Son to George Imlay, resident in Aberdeen, app to Geo Craig,
    shoemaker, 5 years after 1 July 1777.   The father and John Gambel,
    vintner, cautioners.
Imray, Robert   4 May 1793
    Son of Robert Imray, cowfeeder in Gilcomston, app to James Roust,
    wright, 5 years after Whitsunday 1788.   Fee £4.   The father caut.

Ingram, Alexander   30 Apr 1790
    Son of John Ingram, labourer at the brickilns near Aberdeen,
    apprenticed to George Watson, baker, 5 years after Martinmas 1785.
    Fee £5.   The father, Adam Ingram, labourer at the brickilns and
    Francis Gerard, stabler, cautioners.
Izat, David   3 Jun 1793
    Son of the late D. Izat, Shipmaster in Aberdeen, apprenticed to
    James Gordon and Co goldsmiths, 7 years from 13 Jun 1786.   No fee.
    Ar. Gibbon, shipbuilder in Footdee, cautioner.

J

Jaffrey, Andrew   28 Feb 1755
    Son to the late Andrew Jaffrey in Kosienook, apprenticed to Robert
    Joyner, tailor, 8 years after 22 May 1747, no fee.
James, John   12 Feb 1795
    Son of the late Thomas James in Kincardine, apprenticed to William
    Strachan, baker, 5 years after 15 May 1791.   Fee £5.   William Dunn,
    merchant in Aberdeen, cautioner.
Jamieson, John   2 May 1785
    Son to William Jamieson, farmer in Aberdeen, apprenticed to George
    Strachan, shoemaker, 5 years from 12 Jun 1780.   Fee £3 stg.
Johnston, John   5 Apr 1771
    Son to William Johnston in Old Deer, apprenticed to Alexander Still,
    butcher, 5 years from 10 Jan 1770.   William Neilson, butcher,
    cautioner.   Fee £5 stg, and a bedding of clothes.
Johnston, John   12 Nov 1794
    Son to James Johnston, in Bogfairlie, apprenticed to William Seaton,
    baker, 5 years after 1 Nov 1791.   No fee.   The father cautioner.
Johnston, John   1 Dec 1794
    Son to James Johnston, in Bogfairley, apprenticed to William Seton,
    baker, 5 years after 1 Jul 1793.   No fee.   The father cautioner.
Johnston, Samuel   18 May 1780
    Son of the late James Johnston, late farmer in Kinder, apprenticed to
    Robert Lamb, merchant, 4 years after 1 Jun 1776.   John Forbes,
    shoemaker in Aberdeen, cautioner.
Johnston, William   13 Jun 1789
    Son of the late John Johnston late farmer in the parish of Dyce,
    apprenticed to Ninian Johnston, merchant, 4 years from 21 Jun 1785.
    Fee £10.   Alexander Dyce, merchant in Aberdeen, cautioner.
Joyner, Daniel   26 Sep 1754
    Son to Jerom Joyner, shoemaker in Cromarty, apprenticed to Robert
    Joyner, tailor, 8 years after 8 Sep 1746, no fee.

Joyner, Robert   29 Jul 1752
    Son to Jerom Joyner, shoemaker in Cromarty, apprenticed to Robert
    Joyner, tailor, 6 years after 8 Sep 1746, no fee.

K

Keith, William   30 Nov 1791
    Son of John Keith in the parish of Peterculter apprenticed to John
    Hector, tailor, 5 years from 1 Mar 1787. Fee £5 stg. The father
    and Alexander Buchan, stocking frame smith, cautioners.

Keith, William   16 Oct 1795
    Son to George Keith, shoemaker, app to James Bonnar, clock and
    watchmaker, 5 years after 29 Mar 1791. Fee £10. The father caut.

Kemlo, William   5 Oct 1793
    Son of John Kemlo, weaver in Gilcomston, apprenticed to George Sim,
    saddler and harness maker, 5 years from 5 Dec 1788. No fee. The
    father and Andrew Wilson, wright, cautioners.

Kemp, George   10 Aug 1762
    Son to William Kemp in Gilcomston, apprenticed to Francis Gordon,
    shoemaker, 5 years after 2 Nov 1757, no fee; William Ritchie in
    Gilcomston and the father cautioners.

Kiloh, Alexander   12 May 1789
    Son to John Kiloh in Mains of Elrick, apprenticed to John Smith,
    wright, 5 years from Whitsunday 1784. Fee 10.

Knowles, James   23 May 1787
    Son of William Knowles at Mill of Collairly in the parish of Echt,
    apprenticed to Adam Watt, baker, 5 years from 19 May 1786. Fee £5
    stg, the father and William Chalmers in Easter Collairly, cautioners.

L

Laing, Alexander   9 Nov 1791
    Son to James Laing, resident in Aberdeen, apprenticed to George
    Stott, weaver, 5 years from 1 Dec 1786. No fee. The father and
    John Gilchrist, in Aberdeen, cautioners.

Laing, Peter   10 Dec 1792
    Son to James Laing, resident in Aberdeen, apprenticed to John Milne,
    weaver, 6 years from 10 Dec 1792. No fee. Cautioners, the father
    and John Gilchrist, resident.

Law, James   11 Jun 1771
    Son to John Law, wright in Aberdeen, apprenticed to James Gordon,
    jeweller goldsmith, 6 years after 8 Jul 1765. The father and
    Alexander Inglis, blacksmith, cautioners.

Law, William   21 Dec 1795
    Grandson of John Law, wright, one of the boys educated in Robert
    Gordon's Hospital, with consent of Elizabeth Law, his sister, James
    Smith, maltman, and John Copland, treasurer of the Hospital,
    apprenticed to Alexander Tytler, shoemaker, 5 years after 25 Dec
    1790.   Fee £100 Scots.   The above James Smith cautioner.
Ledingham, George   1 Aug 1761
    Son to Jas Ledingham, farmer in Old Lesley, app to Wm Duguid,
    merchant, 5 years after 11 May 1761.   Fee 13 1/2 bolls of meal at 9
    stone, 3 1/2 bolls at Candlemas next, and 2 1/2 bolls for each of the
    4 subsequent years at Candlemas, with a bedding of clothes.
Legate, John   2 Mar 1773
    Son to George Legate in Mains of Byth, apprenticed to John Lamb,
    wright, 6 years after 1 Jul 1770.
Legg, George   22 Mar 1783
    Son to the late Peter Legg, late wright in Aberdeen, apprenticed to
    John Lamb, wright, one of the boys educated in Robert Gordon's
    Hospital, with consent of Helen Collie, alias Legg, his mother, and Mr
    John Copland, present treasurer of the said Hospital, 5 years after 1
    Jun 1778.   Fee £100 Scots.   Patrick Baron of Woodside, cautioner.
Legget, Theophilus   13 Mar 1792
    Son to ? Legget in Greinhall, app to John Low, tailor, 7 years from 24
    May 1787.   No fee.   Theophilus Ogilvie Esq of Greinhall, cautioner.
Leighton, Thomas   2 Feb 1787
    Son to Patrick Leighton, merchant in Aberdeen, apprenticed to
    Messrs William and James Young, manufacturers, 5 years after
    Candlemas 1782.   Fee £100 Scots, payable by the Treasurer of
    Robert Gordon's Hospital.   The father, as cautioner, to maintain his
    son in bed, board, washing, clothes and all other necessaries.
Leighton, William   4 Apr 1778
    Son to Peter Leighton, manufacturer in Aberdeen, apprenticed to
    James Clerk, tailor, 7 years after Whitsunday 1771.   The father and
    Archibald Leighton, bookbinder in Aberdeen, cautioners.
Leiper, John   4 Oct 1787
    Son of late Alex Leiper, mariner in Aberdeen, one of the boys of
    Gordon's Hospital, apprenticed to Alex Tytler, shoemaker, 5 years
    after 26 Oct 1782.   Fee £100 Scots.   James Mathew, mariner, caut.
Leitch, William   2 May 1785
    Son to Wm Leitch, woolcomber in Aberdeen, one of the boys educated
    in Robert Gordon's Hospital, app to Messrs Hugh Gordon & Co, 7 years
    from 8 Feb 1779.   Fee £100 Scots.   The apprentice to maintain
    himself in bed, board and clothing.   John Young, merchant, caut.

Leith, Alexander   11 Dec 1789
    Son of John Leith, post in Old Meldrum, app to Wm Seton, baker, 5yrs
    from 3 jun 1785, fee £4. Father and Rbt Milne, Bridge of Don, cauts.
Leith, John   13 Sep 1785
    Son to William Leith, farmer in Cromar, apprenticed to John Leith,
    coppersmith, 5 years from Candlemas 1781.   No fee, the master to
    provide bed and board.   John Smith, pewterer, cautioner.
Levie, William   7 Mar 1793
    Son to Wm Levie, sailor, app to Geo Strachan, shoemaker, 6 years
    from 1 Apr 1788.   No fee, the father and John Smith, labourer, cauts.
Leys, William   26 Oct 1784
    Son to Francis Leys at Inver Aberarder, parish of Crathy, apprenticed
    to Alexander Morison, cooper, 5 years from 15 May 1783.   Fee £10
    stg.   Francis Leys in Inverhall, cautioner.
Ligertwood, James   18 Jun 1792
    Son of George Ligertwood in Balmakessie, appr to James Finnie,
    wright, 4 years from 20 Jun 1788.   Fee £12 10s.   Father cautioner.
Ligertwood, Thomas   2 Feb 1787
    Son of the late Alexander Ligertwood, late farmer in Chapeltown,
    with consent of William Duncan, schoolmaster, as cautioner,
    apprenticed to James Niell, weaver, 5 years after 14 Nov 1782.
Low, Adam   16 Mar 1795
    Son to William Low, Wardhouse, apprenticed to Margaret Kennedy,
    baker, relict of the late John Morice, baker, 3 years after 7 Nov
    1794.   No fee.   The father cautioner.
Low, Robert   18 Apr 1785
    Son to Robert Low, farmer in Balfigh in the parish of Fordon,
    apprenticed to James Murray, baker, 5 years from 4 Dec 1780.
Lumsden, Benjamin   20 Aug 1786
    Son to Benjamin Lumsden, goldsmith in Aberdeen, apprenticed to
    James Gordon and Co, goldsmiths, 4 years after 26 Sep 1782.   No
    fee.   The apprentice to uphold himself in bed and board, and his
    masters to pay him £1 10s in name of board wages.
Lumsden, David   6 Mar 1775
    Son to John Lumsden in Boghead, apprenticed to Thomas Abel, baker,
    5 years after 2 Jun 1771.
Lumsden, Harry   8 Oct 1760
    Son to William Lumsden in Mid Clova, app to Adam Baxter, cooper, 6
    years after Aug 1755, fee £10. 10s stg with a bedding of clothes.
Lunan, Charles   5 Apr 1771
    Son to the late William Lunan in Monymusk, apprenticed to Hugh
    Gordon, clock and watchmaker, 6 years after 20 Mar 1766.   James
    Thain, blacksmith in Aberdeen, cautioner.

Lyell, James   28 Nov 1792
  Son of Alexander Lyell in Loch Eye, apprenticed to R Johnston,
  blacksmith, 5 years from 8 Apr 1788.   No fee.   Cautioners, the
  father and Alexander Strath in Lochhead.

M

Machray, Robert   3 Nov 1788
  Son to William Machray, waulker at Walkmill of Bendach,
  app to James Crombie, dyer in Gilcomston, 5 years from 5 Dec 1783.
  No fee.   The father and Robert Machray, dyer in Aberdeen, caut.
Machray, Robert   12 Feb 1795
  Son of Robert Machray, dyer in Old Aberdeen, app to William Donald,
  baker, 5 years after 14 Feb 1790.   Fee £6.   The father cautioner.
Mackie, William   18 May 1784
  Son to Peter Mackie in Muchals, apprenticed to David Walker, cooper,
  5 years after 1 Jun 1781.   Fee £10 stg and a bedding of clothes.
Mackintosh, Robert   25 Apr 1760
  Son to William Mackintosh, resident in Aberdeen, apprenticed to
  Thomas Simson, butcher, 5 years after 3 May 1759, no fee.
Mair, James   31 Apr 1796
  Son to James Mair, labourer, apprenticed to Joseph Berrie, weaver, 5
  years after 20 Sep 1791.   No fee.   The father cautioner.
Mair, John   23 Jul 1778
  Son to late James Mair in Scurdarg, app to Jas Gordon, jeweller and
  goldsmith, 7 years after 31 Oct 1776.   George Mair, Scurdarg caut.
Machray, George   4 May 1790
  Son of Robert Machray, dyer in Old Aberdeen, apprenticed to Margaret
  Morice and Company, 5 years from 1 May 1789.   Fee £8.   The father
  and Alexander Thomson at Stocket Brae, cautioners.
Marnoch, James   11 Jun 1771
  Son to James Marnoch in Mill of Coynach, app to Robert Morison,
  baker, 5 years after 1 Jan 1771.   Fee £5 stg and bedding of clothes.
Marnoch, Nicholas   5 Apr 1771
  Son to James Marnoch at Mill of Coynoch, apprenticed to Andrew
  Donald, merchant, 5 years from 16 Apr 1770.   The father to
  maintain him in back and body clothes and the master in bed and
  board, working clothes and shoes.
Marr, William   19 Jan 1775
  Son of the late John Marr, butcher in Aberdeen, apprenticed to James
  Brands, tailor, with the consent of his mother, Elisabeth Lindsay, 6
  years from 9 May 1769.   John Reith, tailor in Aberdeen, cautioner.

23

Marr, William   1 Mar 1785

Son of Alex Marr, butcher in Aberdeen, app to Wm Farquharson, saddler, 6 1/2 yrs from Martinmas 1778. Consent of John Copland, Treasurer of Robert Gordon's Hospital, who undertakes to pay the fee of £100Scots in respect of Marr being a boy educated at the hospital.

Martin, Alexander   23 Jul 1778

Son to Alex Martin at Mill of Murtle, app to Alex Martin, butcher, 5 years after 11 Jun 1778. James Allan, merchant in Aberdeen, caut.

Martin, William   12 May 1789

Son to John Martin, in Kirktown in Nether Banchory, apprenticed to John Imray, baker, 5 years from 19 Jun 1784. Fee £5.

Massie, James   15 Jan 1789

Son of Robert Massie, late maltster in Aberdeen, apprenticed to John Ross, baker, 5 years from 1 Feb 1785. Fee £4. James Jaffray and George Jaffray, both wrights, cautioners.

Mathers, David   13 Oct 1792

Son to David Mathers at Coulter, apprenticed to David Barclay, shoemaker, 5 years from 1 Nov 1787. Fee £2 stg. Father cautioner.

Mathieson, Alexander   17 Mar 1791

Son to William Mathieson, woolcomber, apprenticed to George Adam, shoemaker, 5 years from 15 May 1786. Fee £2 10s.

Matthew, John   –   1 Sep 1793

Son of Alexander Matthew, shoemaker in Logie, apprenticed to George Watson, baker, 5 years after Martinmas 1789. Fee £5. The father and Robert Vass, stabler in Aberdeen, cautioners.

McCombie, George   18 May 1796

Son of the late George McCombie, sometime in Newbigging, app to Alex Dalgarno, merchant, 5 years after 21 Jun 1791. No fee. Rev Robert Farquharson, Minister of Coldstone, cautioner.

McCraw, Charles   17 Mar 1784

Son of the late ? McCraw, apprenticed to John Low, tailor, 7 years after Martinmas 1777, no fee. No cautioner.

McDonald, Daniel   14 Dec 1784

Son to the late Archibald McDonald, resident in Aberdeen, apprenticed to George Forbes jr, tailor, 7 years from 1 Jan 1778. No fee. Alexander McDonald, woolcomber, cautioner.

McDonald, Donald   2 Jan 1778

Son to Farquhar McDonald, hatdresser in Aberdeen, app to James Simson, tailor, 5 years from 4 Jul 1775. Fee £5 stg. The father and Professor Roderick McLeod of the King's College, cautioners.

McKay, Andrew   4 Apr 1778

Son to Hugh McKay, dancing master in Aberdeen, apprenticed to Joseph Forbes, wright, 5 years after 6 Apr 1778.

McKay, Hugh   4 Apr 1778
    Son to Hugh McKay, dancing master in Aberdeen, apprenticed to
William Duncan, wright, 5 years after 27 Mar 1778.

McKay, Thomas   11 May 1781
    Son of the late James McKay, farmer in Scrapehard, apprenticed to
Alexander Aberdeen, cooper, 5 years after 15 May 1776. Fee £11
stg. Alexander Gillan in Skene, cautioner.

McKenzie, Alexander   29 Apr 1793
    Son to Duncan McKenzie, quarrier at Skene's Square, app to Wm Bain,
weaver, 5 years after 18 Aug 1793. Fee £2 15s. The father caut.

McKenzie, David   3 Jun 1793
    One of the boys in the Poor's Hospital, apprenticed to David Wyllie,
tailor, 6 years from 5 Jun 1786. Fee 10s yearly during
apprenticeship. Daniell Cameron, chaise driver, cautioner.

Melvin, Alexander   6 Apr 1761
    Son to Alex Melvin at Denburn, app to Alex Leighton, shoemaker, 6
years after Whitsunday 1755, fee £3 stg and two pairs of blankets.

Melvin, Peter   5 Nov 1783
    Son to late Wm Melvin in Peterculter, app to Robert Mackie, skinner
and tanner, 5 years after 1 Dec 1778, no fee. James Melvin, salmon
fisher on Dee, and George Melvin, carter at Petmuckston, cauts.

Mennie, James   19 Feb 1789
    Son to the late William Mennie in Blacktapp, apprenticed to Thomson,
cooper, 4 years from 2 Jun 1785. Fee £14. Alexander Lawson,
shoemaker at Gilcomston, cautioner.

Menzies, John   12 Mar 1779
    Son to John Menzies shoemaker in Spithill, app to Andrew Robertson,
staymaker, 8 years from 30 Mar 1771. Fee a bedding of clothes and
£1 stg. The farmer and John Mitchell, vintner, Spithill, cauts.

Mercer, John   1 May 1779
    Son to John Mercer, Kirktown of Tyrie, apprenticed to William
Murray, merchant, 5 years after 3 May 1774.

Merchant, Richard   8 Oct 1760
    Son to James Merchant, resident, apprenticed to William Forbes,
coppersmith, 8 years after Whitsunday 1750, no fee.

Michie, John   6 Feb 1772
    Son to William Michie, labourer in Aberdeen, apprenticed to James
Aikin, shoemaker, 5 1/2 years after 1 Sep 1769. John Menie, lint
dresser at Gordon's Mills Manufactory, cautioner.

Mill, James   31 Oct 1786
    Son to Geo Mill at Castle Fraser, app to Arch Reid, baker, 4 years
after Whitsun 1786. Fee £3 stg, master to maintain him in bed and
board. The father and Peter Hatt, gardener at Castle Fraser, cauts.

Miln, John   1 Dec 1756

Son to James Miln, weaver in Fintray, apprenticed to William Stevenson, weaver, 6 years after 2 Jan 1751, no fee.

Milne, Andrew   15 Mar 1793

Son to John Milne, resident near the Bridge of Don, apprenticed to Nathaniel Burnett, baker, 6 years after 18 Mar 1788. No fee. Alexander Allan, at the brick and tile factory near the Bridge of Don, and James Gibson, farmer in Links, cautioners.

Milne, Charles   1 Aug 1783

Son to John Milne, tobacconist in Aberdeen, apprenticed to James Clark, tailor, 5 years after 2 Aug 1778. Fee £3 stg. The father and Peter Copland, merchant, cautioners.

Milne, James   17 Nov 1780

Son to Robert Milne, blacksmith in Ord, Skeen parish, apprenticed to George Adam, merchant, 4 years after 1 Jan 1777.

Milne, John   17 Aug 1779

Son to John Milne, tobacconist in Aberdeen, apprenticed to Alexander Nicoll, shoemaker, 5 years after 20 Aug 1774. Fee £3 10s. The father and Peter Copland, merchant, cautioners.

Milne, Robert   25 Aug 1796

Son to Robert Milne, shipmaster, app to Geo Sim, saddler and harness maker, 5 years after 1 Nov 1791. No fee. John Elric, tidewaiter, caut.

Milne, Thomas   5 Nov 1783

Son to the late William Milne, farmer in Gillowhill, apprenticed to Robert Mackie, skinner, 5 years after 11 Oct 1781. No fee. James Aiken, shoemaker in Aberdeen, cautioner.

Milne, William   2 Feb 1786

Son of the late John Milne, farmer in Cotswells, app to William Thom, wright, 5 years from 12 Feb 1781. Fee £5 stg. James Milne in Blackpotts and Alexander Barrack in Cotswells, cauts.

Milne, William   1 Mar 1792

Son of George Milne, shoemaker, a boy from Robert Gordon's Hospital, app to Alexander Jopp, cooper, 5 yrs from 6 Oct1787. Fee £100Scots.

Milne, William   1 Jun 1795

Son of Alex Milne at Mill of Grandhome, app to Alex Thomson, cooper, 5 years after 2 Dec 1790. Fee £10. The father cautioner.

Mitchell, George   26 Oct 1792

Son of Joseph Mitchell, vintner, apprenticed to William Littlejohn, wright, 5 years from 28 Apr 1792. Fee £15.

Mitchell, John   4 Apr 1778

Son to Robert Mitchell in Balmoor, nr Peterhead, apprenticed to John Tower, cooper, 5 years after 20 May 1773. Fee £11 stg. The father and James Arbuthnot, merchant in Peterhead, cautioners.

Mitchell, John   15 Oct 1792
    Son to Joseph Mitchell, vintner, apprenticed to Alexander Leslie and
    Co, druggists, 6 years from 1 Aug 1787.   No fee.

Moir, Alexander   29 Apr 1793
    Son to Alex Moir in Cardhillock, parish of Newhills, app to Wm Sang,
    baker, 5 years after 1 May 1793.   No fee.   The father caut.

Moir, George   29 Aug 1787
    Son to John Moir, Mill of Balcairn, app to Andrew Simpson, merchant
    in Aberdeen, 5 years after 2 Sep 1782.   Fee £10, master to maintain
    in bed and board.   The father and Peter Anderson, tailor, cauts.

Moir, George   7 Aug 1793
    Son to Wm Moir in Bendach, parish of Dyce, app to Margaret Morice,
    baker, 5 years after Whitsunday 1791.   Fee £2.   The father caut.

Moir, William   2 Mar 1773
    Son to John Moir in Lochtoun of Kennerty, app to John Lamb, wright,
    5 years from 27 Apr 1763.   Father and Geo Hendry at Kennerty,cauts.

Moir, William   27 Oct 1795
    Son to John Moir, farmer Mill of Balcairn, app to Geo Moir, merchant,
    4 yrs from1 Nov1791, no fee.   Father and Alex Tytler, shoemaker
    cauts.

More, George   23 May 1787
    Son of late Alexander More in Forresterhill, app to James Clark,
    tailor, 5 years after Whitsunday 1783.   Fee £3 stg, master to
    maintain in bed, board & lodging.   Rbt Moir, journeyman tailor, caut.

Morgan, Moses   5 Nov 1777
    Son to William Morgan, blacksmith in Tulloch, apprenticed to
    Alexander Grant, baker, 4 years after 15 Jun 1776, fee £6.

Morice, George   15 Sep 1761
    Son to George Morice in Farburn of Stoniewood, apprenticed to John
    Morice, baker, for 5 years after Whitsunday 1760.   No apprentice
    fee.   Mr William Morice, minister at Caryston, cautioner.

Morice, Thomas   2 May 1785
    Son to John Morice in Grandhome, app to John Lamb, wright, 5 1/2
    years from 7 Nov 1780.   Fee £4 stg, the master to maintain the
    apprentice in bed and board.   John Morice, wright in Old Aberdeen,
    and Alexander Craighead in Buckie of Grandhome, cautioners.

Morison, Alexander   12 Mar 1779
    Son to Gilbert Morison in Stodfold, app to Alex Aberdeen, cooper, 5
    yrs from 24 Mar 1774.   Fee eight guineas and one boll of meal.

Morison, Alexander   30 Oct 1793
    Son to John Morison, wright, apprenticed to Joseph Yule, tailor, 6
    years from 30 Oct 1787.   No fee.   The father cautioner.

Morison, George   20 Aug 1787
> Son to Gilbert Morison in Little Elrick, in the parish of Old Deer, apprenticed to William Morison, merchant, 5 years after 2 Sep 1782. Fee £10 stg, the master to provide bed, board and lodging.

Morison, John   2 Feb 1786
> Son of George Morison, watchmaker, app to his father, 7 years after 26 Feb 1779. No fee. James Hunter, merchant, cautioner.

Morison, William   20 Feb 1788
> Son to the late William Morison in Knocnado, app to Garvock & Whyte, staymakers, 5 years from 28 Apr 1783. No fee. William Innes, lint dresser and James Logie, soap boiler, both in Aberdeen, cautioners.

Morison, William   3 Nov 1788
> Son to the late John Morison, late in Gilcomston, app to Robert Taylor, baker, 5 years from 28 Jun 1787. Fee £5. Archibald Reid, baker, and John Christie, lastwright in Skenes Square, cautioners.

Mortimer, John   22 Oct 1793
> Son of George Mortimer, stabler, apprenticed to John Ross, baker, 5 years from 1 Jan 1789. Fee £5. The father cautioner.

Mortimer, Robert   1 Aug 1783
> Son to Arthur Mortimer in Smiddyhill of Alford, apprenticed to James Masson, baker, 4 years after 1 Jun 1781, fee £8 stg.

Murray, George   4 May 1790
> Son of the late William Murray in Meldrum, apprenticed to Margaret Morice and Company, 5 years from 1 Jun 1785. Fee £8. William Murray, Lochter, Meldrum, cautioners.

Murray, Hugh   19 Aug 1785
> Son of Robert Murray in Cabrach, app to James Hacket, shoemaker, 6 years from 1 Sep 1780. No fee. Alex Henderson in Sand of Craig, cautioner. The master to maintain the apprentice in bed and board.

Murray, John   11 Nov 1778
> Son to John Murray in Belhelvie, apprenticed to James Smith, glazier, 6 years after 25 Nov 1772. The father and William Robertson, tailor in Spitle, cautioners.

N

Napier, John   10 Dec 1764
> Son to the late John Napier in Finnan, apprenticed to Alexander Nicol, shoemaker; 6 years after 15 Nov 1758. Fee £24 Scots. Andrew Napier at Miln of Finnan, cautioner.

Nicoll, Andrew   1 Aug 1783
  Son to Geo Nicoll, tile maker in Aberdeen, to Wm Knowles, wright, 5
  yrs from 25 May 1781. Fee-cautioners to maintain the apprentice in
  board for the first 2 1/2 yrs and in tools for his employment the
  second 2 1/2 years, and a bedding of clothes worth £2 stg. Father,
  Geo Webster at Mr Auldjo's brickwork, Aberdeen and Jas Nicoll,tailor
  in Old Aberdeen, cauts.
Nowall, Alexander   1 Aug 1783
  Son to Alexander Nowall in Cluny, apprenticed to Archibald Reid,
  baker, 6 years after 1 Jun 1780. Fee £5 stg. The father and
  Andrew Robertson, merchant in Aberdeen, cautioners.

O

Ogg, Andrew   29 Jan 1793
  Son to John Ogg, miller at Wierdmill of Drum, in parish of Drumoak,
  apprenticed to William French, baker, 5 years from 9 Aug 1789. Fee
  £5. The father cautioner.
Ogilvie, John   7 Jul 1792
  Son of Alexander Ogilvie, merchant, Loanhead, apprenticed to James
  Christie, saddler, 6 1/2 years from 21 Feb 1786. No fee. The
  father and John Leslie at Steps of Gilcomston, cautioners.
Ogilvie, John   30 Jul 1792
  Son to Rev Dr John Ogilvie at Midmar, apprenticed to William Michie,
  wright, 5 years from 1 Apr 1792. Fee £8 stg. The father cautioner.

P

Paterson, John   6 Jul 1779
  Son to the late Walter Paterson, late in Springfield, apprenticed to
  William French, baker, 5 years after 9 Jul 1774. Fee £6 stg.
  Alexander Paterson, in the parish of Tough, cautioner.
Peterkin, James   24 Nov 1766
  Son to the late William Peterkin in Clackria, apprenticed to John
  Burnet jr, merchant in Aberdeen, 5 years after 1 Dec 1761. No fee,
  but to maintain himself in bed, board and clothing during his
  apprenticeship. William Peterkin, schoolmaster at Doors, cautioner.
  The master to pay his apprentice 2s weekly.
Petrie, James   23 Nov 1791
  Son of the late George Petrie, sheriff officer in Old Aberdeen,
  apprenticed to James Ramsay, tailor, 6 years from 15 Dec 1785.
  Fee £1 for a bedding of clothes. William Williamson, gardener in
  Old Aberdeen, and James Brice, baker, cautioner.

Pirie, Andrew   9 Jun 1793
> Son to Alexander Pirie, wheelwright, apprenticed to James Finnie, wright, 5 years after 11 Jun 1789. Fee £10. The father cautioner.

Porter, James   23 May 1787
> Son of the late Alexander Porter, late in Old Meldrum, apprenticed to William Strachan, baker, 5 years after 1 Jun 1782. Fee £9 stg, the master to maintain him in bed, board and lodging only. George Cruickshank, farmer in Belhagarty, cautioner.

Prott, Arthur   22 Dec 1769
> Son to John Prott, woolcomber in Aberdeen, apprenticed to Alexander Kemlo, shoemaker, 6 years after 7 Dec 1768. The father and John Watt, woolcomber, cautioners, to maintain him in clothes during the indenture and to maintain him in bed and board for a year, which year's bed and board is valued at £3 stg.

R

Rae, William   22 May 1751
> Son to late Wm Rae in Lumphannen, app to James Smith, saddler, 6 years from Whitsun 1746, no fee; Alex Mitchell in Aberdeen, caut.

Rainie, Alexander   4 Apr 1778
> Son to John Rainie at Mill of Gight, apprenticed to Archibald Reid, baker, 5 years after 16 Jun 1775. Fee £6 stg, and a bedding of clothes. William Milne, baker, cautioner.

Ramsay, Archibald   16 Apr 1790
> Son of Samuel Ramsay tidesman, Aberdeen, app to Jas Ramsay, tailor 6 yrs fm 10 May 1784, fee £1. Father and John Smith tidesman, cauts.

Reid, Alexander   1 Mar 1796
> Son of Alexander Reid in Mains of Barra, app to James Finnie, wright, 5 years after 10 Feb 1792. Fee £11. The father cautioner.

Reid, George   6 Jul 1779
> Son to the late William Reid, weaver in Aberdeen, apprenticed to William Stevenson, weaver, 5 years from Martinmas 1774. George Chapman, weaver in Aberdeen, cautioner.

Reid, John   2 Jan 1778
> Son to Robert Reid in Newburgh, apprenticed to Alexander Cruickshank, shoemaker, 5 years from Martinmas 1777, fee £4 stg.

Reid, William   18 May 1784
> Son to John Reid in Easter Mains of Auchinhove, app to David Walker, cooper, 5 years after 1 Apr 1780. Fee £10 and a bedding of clothes.

Reith, Robert   12 Oct 1791
> Son of John Reith, tailor in Aberdeen, apprenticed to William Dunn, merchant, 5 years from 22 Nov 1786. No fee. John Reith cautioner.

Rhind, John   29 Jul 1751
    Son to John Rhind, mason, app to George Wright, cooper, 6 years
    after Whitsun 1748; previously app to Gilbert Duff, cooper - no fee.
Riach, Peter   20 Dec 1791
    Son to Harry Riach in Minmore, parish of Cushnie, apprenticed to
    John Wallalce, baker, 5 years from 5 Jan 1787. Fee £5 stg. The
    father and Alexander Duncan, merchant, cautioners.
Riddel, Donaldson   4 Jun 1792
    Son of John Riddel at Windmill brae, apprenticed to George Beet,
    blacksmith, 5 years from Martinmas 1789. The father cautioner.
Riddell, David   30 Jun 1790
    Son to Wm Riddell, cobbler, Aberdeen, app to Geo Strachan,shoe-
    maker, 5 years from 22 Aug 1785. Apprentice to maintain himself
    for first 15 months. Father and Jas Farquhar, shoemaker, cauts.
Robb, Andrew   4 May 1790
    Son of John Robb, overseer of the salmon fishings at Nether Don,
    app to Margaret Morice & Company, 5 years from 1 Jan1789, fee £7.
Robertson, Colin   11 Dec 1789
    Son of late Geo Robertson, late merchant, a boys of Robert Gordon's
    Hospital, app to John Leslie, goldsmith, 5 yrs from 1 Feb1785. fee
    £100Scots, Anne Allan, his mother, and Jas Gordon, goldsmith, cauts.
Robertson, Francis   25 Jan 1791
    Son of George Robertson, late merchant, a Gordon's Hospital boy, app
    to Lewis Wilson, tailor, 5 years from 2 May 1786. Fee   £100
    Scots. Anne Allan, his mother, and James Gordon, goldsmith, cauts.
Robertson, George   7 Jul 1792
    Son of George Robertson, burgess, one of the boys of Robert Gordon's
    Hospital, apprenticed to William Farquharson, saddler, 5 years from
    22 Aug 1787. Fee £100 Scots. James Gordon, jeweller, and the
    apprentice's mother, Ann Allan, cautioners.
Robertson, James   7 Aug 1766
    Son to late John Robertson in Annachie of Birse, app to Thomas
    Robertson, weaver, 5 years after Martinmas 1762. Fee a boll of
    meal and bedding of clothes. Alex Collie, shoemaker, Hardgate, caut.
Robertson, John   26 Sep 1760
    Son to Thomas Robertson, app to Alex Leighton, weaver, 6 years and
    1 year after 17 Aug 1733. £8 Scots paid as fee by Session.
    Indenture assigned to Robert Lamb, weaver, on Leighton's death.
Robertson, John   13 Aug 1788
    Son to William Robertson, tailor in Spittal, apprenticed to John
    Murray, glazier, 6 years from 5 August 1783. No fee. The father
    and Peter Robertson, staymaker, cautioners.

Robertson, Thomas   23 May 1787
    Son of James Robertson, weaver, apprenticed to William Strachan,
    baker, 5 years from Jul 1784. Fee £8 6s 8d stg, the master to
    maintain in bed and board only. The father and the Treasurer of
    Robert Gordon's Hospital, cautioners.
Robertson, William   10 Jun 1762
    Son to the late Alexander Robertson, farmer in Glenistown of
    Culsalmond, apprenticed to William Lesley, merchant, 3 years after
    Whitsun 1760. No fee. John Lesley, merchant in Aberdeen, caut.
Robertson, William   13 Feb 1784
    Son to William Robertson, tailor in Spittall, apprenticed to Peter
    Robertson, staymaker, 5 years after 16 Apr 1779, no fee. The
    father and James Allan, farmer in Spittall, cautioners.
Roger, Alexander   13 Oct 1785
    Son of George Roger, farmer in Tillieangus, in the parish of Clatt,
    apprenticed to James Gordon, jeweller goldsmith, 7 years from
    Martinmas 1778. No fee.
Roger, George   11 Jun 1771
    Son to James Roger, stabler, apprenticed to James Gordon, jeweller
    goldsmith, 7 years from 18 Aug 1766. The father and Thomas
    Simson elder, butcher, cautioners.
Roger, Thomas   26 Sep 1760
    Son to James Roger, stabler, apprenticed to William Forbes,
    coppersmith, 9 years after Lammas 1758, no fee.
Ronald, Harry   18 May 1784
    Son to James Ronald in Bogstrype, apprenticed to John Forbes,
    shoemaker, 5 years after 3 Jun 1779. Fee £6 10s.
Ronald, James   11 Aug 1791
    Son to James Ronald, farmer in Boghead, apprenticed to George Gibb,
    cooper, 5 years from 26 Aug 1785. Fee £12 stg. The father and Mr
    John Ronald, preacher of the Gospel, cautioners.
Ronald, William   13 Feb 1792
    Son of William Ronald, farmer in Boghead of Auchindore, apprenticed
    to Alexander Thomson, cooper, 5 years from 20 Mar 1787. Fee £10.
Ross, Alexander   1 Mar 1792
    Son of Finlay Ross, residing in Aberdeen, apprenticed to Peter
    Duncan, weaver, 5 years from 8 Jun 1787. No fee. The father and
    Hugh Ross sen, cautioners.
Ross, Alexander   27 Apr 1793
    Son to Robert Ross, staymaker in Elgin, apprenticed to Peter
    Robertson, staymaker, 5 years from 17 May 1788. No fee. The
    father and James Davie, woolcomber in Aberdeen, cautioners.

Ross, Alexander   28 Sep 1795
    Son of late Alex Ross, in Strathdon, app to William Leys, cooper, 4
    years after 1 Dec 1791. Fee £17, John Forbes in Mains of New, caut.

Ross, David   9 Oct 1780
    Son to Hugh Ross, Town Sergeant in Aberdeen, one of the boys
    educated in Robert Gordon's Hospital, with consent of Baillie James
    Cruickshank present Treasurer of the said Hospital, app to Magnus.

Ross, George   12 Feb 1795
    Son of Alexander Ross, carter to Strachan, Imray and Company at
    New Bridge, apprenticed to William Strachan, baker, 7 years after 12
    Aug 1788. No fee. The father cautioner.

Ross, James   8 Sep 1760
    Son to John Ross, resident, app to John Jaffrey, weaver, 6 years
    after Martinmas 1755.   No fee, master to pay app £5 Scots yearly.

Rust, James   20 May 1778
    Son to John Rust, late farmer in Dyce, with consent of Alexander
    Rust, farmer, in Hauchhillock; William Rust, farmer in Greenburn;
    and James Bartlet, farmer in Hauchhillock, apprenticed to William
    Knolls, wright, 5 years after 1 Jun 1773. Fee £6 stg. The said
    William Rust and James Bartlet cautioners.

S

Sang, Thomas   31 Apr 1796
    Son to Robert Sang in Green Loan, parish of Kincardine, app to Joseph
    Berrie, weaver, 5 years after 3 Jun 1791. Fee £1. The father caut.

Sangster, George   7 Sep 1768
    Son to the late John Sangster, blacksmith in Aberdeen, apprenticed
    to James Farquhar, shoemaker, 5 years after 11 Sep 1764. Fee £3
    stg, with a bedding of clothes.   Basil Law, wright in Keith caut.

Sangster, John   23 May 1787
    Son of the late Andrew Sangster in Longside, apprenticed to William
    Strachan, baker, 5 years from 19 Jun 1785. Fee £5 stg and a bed and
    a bedding of clothes, the master to maintain in bed, board and
    lodging.   John Moir in Kirktown of Longside, cautioner.

Scott, Alexander   15 Jan 1789
    Son to James Scott, blacksmith, one of the boys educated in Robert
    Gordon's Hospital, apprenticed to George Craig, shoemaker, 5 years
    from 20 Jan 1784. Fee £100 Scots.

Seaton, James   10 Apr 1782
    Son to William Seaton, in Bonnyton in the parish of Undy, apprenticed
    to William Strachan, baker, 5 years from 1 Jun 1780, fee £9 stg.

Shepherd, Alexander   22 Jul 1784
    Son to James Shepherd at Forresterhill, apprenticed to Margaret
    Morice and Company, bakers, 4 years from 1 Sep 1780. Fee £10 stg.
Shepherd, Thomas   12 May 1789
    Son of late Thomas Shepherd, late cooper in Aberdeen, a boy of
    Robert Gordon's Hospital, app to John Smith, wright.   The treasurer
    of the Hospital to pay £100 Scots and Mr James Brands, accountant
    to the Banking Company of Aberdeen, cautioner, to pay £6 13s 4d
    additional.   The apprenticeship to be 5 years from 22 Jun 1784.
Shepherd, William   6 Sep 1789
    Son to George Shepherd at Greenburn, Craibston, apprenticed to
    James Dawney, shoemaker, 5 years from 9 Nov 1784. Fee £2 15s.
Sheriff, David   1 Jun 1781
    Son to Alexander Sheriff in Earles, Aquholly, apprenticed to William
    Donald, baker, 5 years after Whitsunday 1778, fee £7 stg.
Sheriffs, John   15 Apr 1760
    Son to John Sheriffs in Crampston, apprenticed to David Sheriffs,
    wright, 6 years after 27 Jun 1754, fee £4 stg and a bedding of
    clothes and a boll of meal yearly.
Sheriffs, John   11 Jun 1771
    Son to late John Sheriffs, maltster in Aberdeen, a boy educated in
    Robert Gordon's Hospital, app to the Jas Gordon, jeweller goldsmith,
    6 years from 30 May 1768.   Fee £100 Scots, payable by Treasurer of
    the Hospital. Jean Mitchell, mother and Joseph Eggliston cauts.
Silver, Alexander   18 May 1784
    Son of late John Silver in Oldhillock, app to John Smith, wright, 5yrs
    from 21 May1779. Fee £10 stg, Alex Walker, Mill of Montquoich,caut.
Singer, Adam   21 Jan 1783
    Son to James Singer, merchant, parish of Insch, apprenticed to John
    Niven, merchant, 5 years after 4 February 1778.   The father and
    Adam Singer, in Mill of Glanderston, cautioners.
Smith, Alexander   30 Nov 1779
    Son to late James Smith, late one of the doctors of the Grammar
    School of Aberdeen, app to Alexander Ross yr, merchant, 6 years
    after 1 Dec 1773.   John Nicoll, merchant in Aberdeen, caut.
Smith, Alexander   23 Apr 1783
    Son to Wm Smith, blacksmith in Aberdeen, app to Messrs Alexander
    Robertson and John Chalmers, merchants and manufacturers, 5 years
    after 27 Jul 1778.   David Longlands, slater in Aberdeen, cautioner.
Smith, Alexander   3 Mar 1786
    Son to Wm Smith, slater in Aberdeen, app to John Leslie, goldsmith,
    7 yrs from 1 Apr1789.   No fee, but apprentice to maintain himself in
    bed and board for the first year. Father and Jas Smith, glazier,cauts.

Smith, Alexander   2 Feb 1787
    Son of late William Smith, late woolcomber in Aberdeen, app to Alex
    Ferguson, tailor, 6 years from 1 May 1782. Fee, 10s yearly, the
    master to uphold him in bed, board, washing and wearing apparel.
    William Duncan, cashier to the Poor's Hospital of Aberdeen,
    cautioner for the apprentice, who was educated in the said hospital.
Smith, Alexander   27 Nov 1792
    Son to James Smith in Little Clinterty, parish of Newhills,
    apprenticed to Andrew Simpson, merchant, 6 years from 1 Dec 1786.
    No fee.   Cautioners, the father and Alexander Smith, paper
    manufacturer in Mains of Stoneywood.
Smith, Alexander   29 Apr 1793
    Son to Alex Smith, carter in the Schoolhill, app to William Bain,
    weaver, 5 years after 18 Mar 1794.   Fee £4.   The father cautioner.
Smith, George   3 Sep 1784
    Son of the late Robert Smith, slater in Aberdeen, apprenticed to
    James Smith, glazier, 5 years from 17 Sep 1779, no fee.   Patrick
    Urquhart, wright, and John Farquhar, slater, cautioners.
Smith, James   14 Aug 1760
    Son to James Smith, farmer in Aberdeen, apprenticed to John
    Anderson, glazier, 6 years after 9 Nov 1756, no fee.
Smith, James   1 Aug 1783
    Son of the late James Smith in Dubston, parish of Forbes,
    apprenticed to Archibald Reid, baker, 5 years after Whitsunday,
    1779.   Fee £5 stg.   William Smith in Dubston, cautioner.
Smith, John   24 Sep 1791
    Son of the late John Smith, wright in Gilcomston, apprenticed to
    John Lamb, wright, 5 years from 6 Nov 1786.   No fee.   Alexander
    Burnet jr, merchant, cautioner.
Smith, Robert   31 May 1770
    Son to John Smith, quarrier, Aberdeen, with consent of Robert Smith,
    gardener in Hadgate, app to Jas Brands, tailor, 5 years after 11 Jun
    1765, fee £2.10s stg.   The cautioner to maintain the apprentice in
    all necessary wearing apparel and body clothes during the indenture.
Smith, William   6 Mar 1775
    Son to George Smith in Baggerwrath, apprenticed to Thomas Abel,
    baker, 5 years after 11 Sep 1770.
Smith, William
    Son to William Smith in Green Moss, parish of Kemnay, apprenticed
    to Andrew Simpson, merchant, 5 years after 5 Feb 1773.   Fee £5 stg.
    The father and William Gordon, merchant, cautioners.

Smith, William   28 Feb 1780
>Son of John Smith, Millbowie, Skene, app to Wm Strachan, baker, 5 yrs after 11 Feb 1777. Peter Smith, maltman in Aberdeen, caut.

Smith, William   28 Oct 1791
>Son to Wm Smith, slater, app to Peter Robertson, staymaker, 7 years from 9 Dec 1785, no fee. The father and John Murray, glazier, cauts.

Spark, Robert   28 Feb 1780
>Son to James Spark, farmer in Upper Torie, apprenticed to William French, baker, 5 years after 20 Nov 1776. Fee £8 stg.

Spark, Robert   10 Apr 1782
>Son to Thomas Spark, in Tullos, parish of Nigg, apprenticed to Alexander Rhind, merchant, 5 years after 1 May 1777, fee £7 stg.

Spark, William   7 Sep 1790
>Son to Andrew Spark in Overperk, apprenticed to Alexander Davidson, butcher, 5 years after Whitsunday 1789. No fee.

Spring, Andrew   22 Jun 1782
>Son to William Spring, tailor in Aberdeen, apprenticed to John Courage, shoemaker, 7 years after 6 Jun 1775. William Leonard, tailor and John Crombie, baker cautioners.

Spring, Robert   12 Jan 1791
>Son to Robert Spring at Gilcomston, apprenticed to William Strachan, baker, 5 years from 2 Feb 1786. Fee £5.

Stark, George   20 Apr 1779
>Son to Alexander Stark, brewer in Aberdeen, apprenticed to David Walker, cooper, 5 years from 26 May 1774.

Stead, James   26 Nov 1784
>Son to William Stead, mason at Green Burn, apprenticed to William Esslement, baker, 5 years from 8 Dec 1780. Fee £4 stg.

Stead, William   4 Apr 1778
>Son to William Stead in Chapel of Stonnywood, apprenticed to Thomas Abel, baker, 5 years after Martinmas 1775. Fee £6. 10s.

Stephenson, Alexander   24 May 1755
>Son to William Stephenson, resident, apprenticed to Alexander Nicol, shoemaker, 5 years after 28 May 1750, fee £33 Scots; William Stephenson, weaver, cautioner.

Stewart, John   10 Aug 1762
>Son to Rbt Stewart, sometime weaver in Aberdeen, app to John Reid, weaver, 6 yrs after 25 Sept 1760, no fee, Wm Couts, gardener, caut.

Stewart, John   23 May 1787
>Son to James Stewart, late carpenter in Aberdeen, apprenticed to James Clark, tailor, 6 1/2 years after Whitsunday 1781. No fee. Murdoch Macleod, pensioner in Aberdeen, cautioner.

Still, Patrick   5 Nov 1777
    Son to Alexander Still, farmer in Cardens, apprenticed to William
    Ritchie, merchant, 4 years after 6 Dec 1773, fee £35 stg.
Still, William   13 Mar 1791
    Younger son to Alexander Still in Strathry, parish of Kinellar,
    apprenticed to William Still, cooper, 5 years from 1 Jan 1787. No
    fee. The father and Patrick Booth, merchant, cautioners.
Stillas, James   3 Nov 1788
    Son of the late Alexander Stillas in Old Meldrum, apprenticed to
    Archibald Reid, baker, 5 years from 2 Jun 1788. Fee £6. William
    Ogilvie, merchant in Old Aberdeen, cautioner.
Stiven, John   3 Dec 1770
    Son to John Stiven in Forresterhill, apprenticed to John Ferguson,
    butcher, 5 years after 22 Nov 1767. Alexander Duffus, butcher,
    cautioner. Master bound to maintain apprentice honestly in bed and
    board and all necessary wearing clothes and shoes.
Strachan, James   12 May 1760
    Son to Robert Strachan, tailor, apprenticed to Robert Joyner, tailor,
    8 years after 11 Jun 1752, no fee.
Strachan, John   1 Feb 1758
    Son to John Strachan, blacksmith, apprenticed to Robert Thom,
    blacksmith, 5 years after 1 Jun 1755, no fee. Apprentice gets £24
    Scots of wages for the last year. John Shepherd at Miln of Finnan
    and John Shepherd at Portlethen, cautioners.
Stronach, James   18 Jul 1780
    Son to James Stronach, glover in Aberdeen, apprenticed to George
    Craig, shoemaker, 5 years after 19 July 1775. The father and
    Robert Stronach, wright in Aberdeen, his brother, cautioners.
Stuart, John P   12 May 1793
    Son to Alex Stuart,Leslie House,parish of Leslie,app to Alex Mitchell,
    merchant, 3 years after 24 Jun 1791, fee £30 stg. The father caut.
Sutherland, Alexander   13 Aug 1788
    Son to late Adam Sutherland, sometime farmer in Berryhill of Old
    Machar, app to Peter Anderson, tailor, 6 years from 1 Sep 1782. Fee
    £3. Wm Sutherland merchant in Udny, uncle to Alexander, caut.
Sutherland, William   16 Apr 1790
    Son of late Adam Sutherland, app to Peter Anderson, tailor, 6 years
    from 1 May 1784, fee £3 and a bedding of clothes. Alex Sutherland,
    tailor, Aberdeen, and Wm Sutherland, merchant, Udny,cauts.
Symers, George   3 Mar 1786
    Son of George Symers, farmer in Torry, apprenticed to George Gibb,
    cooper, 5 years from 20 Mar 1781. Fee £10 stg and a bedding of
    clothes. The father and James Symers in Torry, cautioners.

Symmers, Andrew   30 Apr 1790
    Son to Wm Symmers, porter,Aberdeen app to David Middleton weaver,
    5 yrs from 4 Jun 1785.   Father and John Chrystal, merchant, cauts.

T

Taylor, Andrew   24 Sep 1787
    Son of the late Andrew Taylor in Culture, apprenticed to Alexander
    Milne, baker, 5 years after 15 Mar 1784.   Fee £5 10s and two pairs
    of blankets.   John Milne in Craigtown, cautioner.
Taylor, James   2 Aug 1766
    Son to David Taylor at Denburn, app to Francis Gordon, shoemaker, 5
    years from date.   The father to give a bedding of clothes and
    maintain him in board and diet for the first half-year, and provide
    wearing clothes during the whole space.   Master to maintain him in
    bed an board during the remaining time, and a pair of shoes yearly.
Taylor, John   29 Jun 1781
    Son to William Taylor in Aberdeen, apprenticed to George Beet,
    blacksmith, 5 years after 1 Jul 1776.   Patrick Brown cautioner.
Taylor, Peter   7 Mar 1793
    Son to the late John Taylor, farmer in ?, apprenticed to James Clark,
    tailor, 7 years after 28 Mar 1787.   No fee.   Alexander Thomson,
    mason and Alexander Wilson, woolcomber, cautioners.
Taylor, Robert   12 Sep 1777
    Son to Patrick Taylor in Strathrise, apprenticed to William Miln,
    baker, 5 years after Martinmas 1776, fee £8 stg.
Taylor, William   31 May 1769
    Late servant to John Dingwalll in Cloghill, app to David Smith,
    blacksmith, 5 years after 4 Dec 1764.   No fee.   Geo Copland, wright
    in Cloghill and Alexander Temple, servant to John Dingwall, cauts.
Thomson, Alexander   20 Apr 1779
    Son to the late William Thomson in Culsamon parish, apprenticed to
    Alexander Jopp, cooper, 5 years after 2 Jun 1774.   Fee £9 stg.
    Alexander Mearns, manufacturer in Aberdeen, cautioner.
Thomson, Charles   10 Aug 1762
    Son to Robert Thomson, resident in Aberdeen, apprenticed to John
    Revels, weaver, 6 years after Whitsunday 1760, no fee
Thomson, Edward   13 Feb 1784
    Son to Charles Thomson, weaver in Aberdeen, apprenticed to William
    Fyfe, tailor, 5 years after 16 Mar 1779.   Fee £2 stg, a chaff bed, a
    pair of blankets and a single sheet.
Thomson, John   24 Jul 1751
    Son to James Thomson, apprenticed to George Wright, cooper.

Thomson, John   28 Sep 1793
   Son of late Jas Thomson, late farmer at Forresterhill, app to Peter
   Robertson, staymaker, 6 yrs from 1 Oct 1787. Fee £5, John Christie,
   chaisemaker, Skene's Square, and Duncan McKenzie, quarrier, cauts.
Thomson, William   1 Feb 1758
   Son to James Thomson, messenger in Aberdeen, apprenticed to John
   Ferguson, cooper, 5 years after Martinmas 1753, no fee.
Tilleray, John   24 Sep 1791
   Son of the late John Tilleray, farmer in Aberdeen, app to John Lamb,
   wright, 5 years after 20 Jan 1789. Fee £8 stg. James Shand, caut.
Tocher, James   11 Mar 1788
   Son to George Tocher in Fyvie, apprenticed to Robert Johnston,
   blacksmith, 5 years from 4 Jun 1784. No fee. The father and John
   Farquhar in Limehillock, Grange, cautioners.
Tough, Charles   5 Nov 1783
   Son to the late Alexander Tough, weaver in Aberdeen, apprenticed to
   John Revells, weaver, 6 years after Candlemas 1778. No fee.
   Alexander Kaird, horner in Aberdeen, cautioner.
Tough, Henry   1 Aug 1783
   Son to the late Henry Tough, resident in Aberdeen, apprenticed to
   David Walker, cooper, 6 years after 1 Sep 1777. No fee. Moses
   Tough, servant to John Norie, painter in Aberdeen, cautioner.
Troup, Benjamin   13 Sep 1785
   Son to Matthew Troup, musician in Aberdeen, app to Andrew Simson,
   shoemaker, 5 years after 14 Sep 1780. No fee, master to provide
   bed and board. The father and Jonathan Troup, his son, cauts.
Troup, John   2 Feb 1786
   Son to James Troup, woolcomber in Aberdeen, apprenticed to George
   Beet, blacksmith, 4 years after 1 Mar 1782. No fee, the apprentice
   to uphold himself in everything.
Troup, John   5 Oct 1793
   Son to the late John Troup, blacksmith in the parish of Banchory,
   apprenticed to George Beet, blacksmith, 5 years from 28 Nov 1788.
   No fee. George Troup, square wright in the parish of Banchory, and
   William Reid, farmer in the parish of Old Machar, cautioners.
Turner, Thomas Andrew   12 Feb 1795
   Son of Robert Turner, Sheriff Substitute of Aberdeen, app to Thomas
   Bannerman, merchant, 4 yrs after 15 Apr 1791, no fee. Father caut.
Turriff, Thomas   14 Dec 1784
   Son to David Turriff, Town Sergeant in Aberdeen, app to John Ewan,
   merchant, 5 yrs from 18 Jan 1783, with the consent of John Copland,
   Treasurer of Robert Gordon's Hospital, who undertakes to pay the fee
   £100 Scots in respect Turriff, a boy educated in said Hospital.

W

Walker, Alexander   22 Jul 1784
Son to the late Peter Walker in Newbiggin, apprenticed to Margaret
Morice and Company, bakers, 4 years from 1 May 1784. Fee £8 stg.
William Walker in Haugh of Glenkindy, cautioner.

Walker, John   18 May 1780
Son to Robert Walker, saddler in Aberdeen, app to George Strachan,
shoemaker, 6 years after 1 Sep 1774. Fee, the father to maintain
his son in bed and board during the two first years, and in washing
during the whole period, and to pay 10s stg for a bedding of clothes.

Walker, John   11 Dec 1782
Son to William Walker, gardener at Gilcomston, apprenticed to
Alexander Aberdeen, cooper, 5 years after 6 Jan 1778. Fee £10 10s
stg and a sufficient bedding of clothes.

Walker, Robert   28 Aug 1782
Son to Andrew Walker,New Mill of Glenbervie, app to Wm Strachan,
baker, 5 years after 15 Jun 1781, fee £6 stg and bedding of clothes.

Walker, William   3 Nov 1788
Son to James Walker in ?, app to Adam Watt, baker, 4 years from 20
Nov 1784. Fee £6. The father and John Walker, auctioneer, cauts.

Wallace, Alexander   2 Jan 1795
Son of Alexlander Wallace, butcher, one of the boys educated in
Robert Gordon's Hospital, apprenticed to James Finnie, wright, 5
years after 11 Jan 1790. Fee £100 Scots on behalf of the Hospital.

Wallace, John   7 Sep 1768
Son to Alexander Wallace, stabler in Aberdeen, apprenticed to
Alexander Miln, baker, 5 years after date. Fee £7 1s stg. The
father and Alexander Lumsden advocate, cautioners.

Warrack, Thomas   24 Mar 1781
Son to John Warrack at Mill of Towie, apprenticed to Morice and Co,
bakers, 5 years after 1 May 1776. Fee £11 stg. The father and
James Warrack in Kildrummy, cautioners.

Watson, James   31 Oct 1786
Son to James Watson, resident in Aberdeen, apprenticed to Archibald
Reid, baker, 5 years after Whitsunday 1784. Fee £5 stg. His
master to maintain him in bed and board. The father, Alexander
Farquhar, merchant, and Alexander Gray, workman, cautioners.

Watson, Joseph   11 May 1789
Son to Wm Watson, tacksman in Caweyford, parish of Old Deer, app
to Alex Mitchell, merchant, 4 years from 22 Jun 1785. Fee £12.
The father and John Todd, weaver in Pittmark house, Old Deer, cauts.

Watson, Robert   30 Apr 1790
    Residing in Aberdeen, apprenticed to Margaret Morice, baker, 5 years
    from 1 Apr 1786. Fee £8.

Watt, Alexander   6 Jul 1779
    Son to Alexander Watt, woolcomber in Aberdeen, apprenticed to
    William Bain, weaver, 5 years from 11 Sep 1777.

Watt, James   2 Feb 1786
    Son to late James Watt in Pitmuckston, app to Alex Martin, butcher,
    5 years after Whitsunday 1784.   George Allan, tailor, cautioner.

Watt, John   5 Nov 1777
    Son to late Chas Watt, woolcomber in Aberdeen, app to David Walker,
    cooper, 6 1/2 years after 6 Nov 1776.   John Rudiman, wright, caut.

Watt, William   11 Feb 1762
    Son to the late Nathaniel Watt in Strathdon, apprenticed to John
    Jaffray, weaver, 5 years after Whitsunday 1761. No fee.   William
    Reid, farmer, Milntown of Glenbucket, cautioner.

Webster, Alexander   11 Dec 1782
    Son to William Webster, weaver in Kincardine, apprenticed to
    Alexander Fiddes, weaver, 5 years after 1 Jan 1778.

Will, Alexander   16 Apr 1793
    Son to the late Andrew Will at Broadford, apprenticed to John Gartly,
    clock and watchmaker, 6 years after 20 Apr 1788. No fee.   George
    Ferrier, candlemaker, cautioner.

Williamson, Alexander   18 Dec 1761
    Son to John Williamson at Fottiesmyre, apprenticed to William
    Leonard, tailor, 6 years after Lammas 1760. No fee.   Thomas
    Simson sen, butcher, cautioner.

Wilson, Charles   20 Feb 1788
    Son to Andrew Wilson, late farmer in Tillieriach, in Tough,
    apprenticed to William French, baker, 5 years from 11 May 1783.
    Fee £6 stg.   Alexander Elmslie, in Wester Lochel, parish of Lochel
    and James Wilson, in Tillieriach of Tough, cautioners.

Wilson, George   1 Aug 1783
    Son to John Wilson, late hecklemaker in Aberdeen, apprenticed to
    William Allan, clock and watchmaker, 5 years after 7 Oct 1778.   Fee
    £5 stg and a bedding of clothes.   William Gavin, tailor, and George
    Michie, resident in Aberdeen, cautioners.

Wilson, James   12 May 1789
    Son of Peter Wilson, weaver in Aberdeen, apprenticed to William
    Leighton, tailor, 5 years from 2 Aug 1785.   The father to maintain in
    bed and board the first year of the apprenticeship.

Wishart, Alexander   23 May 1787
  Son to Wm Wishart in Tarbothill, parish of Belhelvie, app to John
  Tower, cooper, 5 years after 7 Dec 1784.   Fee £10 stg.

Y

Young, James   23 May 1787
  Son of James Young, in New Mill of Crimond, in the parish of
  Keithhall, apprenticed to William Law, baker, 5 years after 4 Nov
  1785.   Fee £4 stg, the master to maintain him in bed and board only.
  The father and John Young, merchant in Aberdeen, cautioners.

www.ingramcontent.com/pod-product-compliance
Lightning Source LLC
Chambersburg PA
CBHW071137280326
41935CB00010B/1268